24136

DATE DUE			
NOV. 26 2007			
APR 0 1 2017			

FAITH & DOUBT

AN ANTHOLOGY OF POEMS

EDITED BY

Patrice Vecchione

HENRY HOLT AND COMPANY • NEW YORK

Charlotte Raymond's got what it takes; she gives it to my projects, and I'm grateful. My thanks to Marion Silverbear, whose assistance extends far beyond permission requests. Thanks, as ever and always, to Michael Stark, aka L.B. At a moment's notice, Anna Paganelli and Elliot Ruchowitz-Roberts came through; thanks for that and much more. The reference librarians at the Monterey Public Library are stellar, and have once again made it possible for my book to shine. Susan Renison of the Watsonville Public Library drove through a late-night downpour for a biography—what a librarian will do! Thanks to the San Jose Public Library. Laura Godwin and Kate Farrell, many thanks.

Henry Holt and Company, LLC
Publishers since 1866
175 Fifth Avenue
New York, New York 10010
www.henryholtchildrensbooks.com

Henry Holt® is a registered trademark of Henry Holt and Company, LLC.
Compilation and introduction copyright © 2007 by Patrice Vecchione
All rights reserved.
Distributed in Canada by H. B. Fenn and Company Ltd.

Library of Congress Cataloging-in-Publication Data
Faith and doubt : an anthology of poems / edited by Patrice Vecchione.—1st ed.
p.   cm.
Includes bibliographical references.
ISBN-13: 978-0-8050-8213-5
ISBN-10: 0-8050-8213-1
1. Poetry—Collections. 2. Belief and doubt—Poetry. I. Vecchione, Patrice.
PN6101.F36 2006
808.81'9382—dc22
                                                        2006018228

First Edition—2007 / Designed by Debbie Glasserman
Printed in the United States of America on acid-free paper. ∞

10 9 8 7 6 5 4 3 2 1
24136

To my father, Nicholas Vecchione,

who continues to teach me the intricacies

of faith and doubt

Contents

FAITH & DOUBT

INTRODUCTION

Just what are you going to believe? What your mother believes? What your father does? What the muscle-y guy down the street or the girl who carries her schoolbooks on top of her head has faith in? Your best friend knows where his faith is located, or so he says. The minister at church sounds convincing. The rabbi has a confidence that's enviable. Your teacher claims to know what's worth believing in. Ancient Greek philosophers said one thing. Confucius another. If the president tells you what to believe, do you automatically believe it? Does his or her faith sway you? Should it? Are you going to believe authority figures because their belief seems more valid than yours? Your favorite song—the one that runs in your mind and lulls you to sleep—sets its belief in harmony, syncopation, or the downbeat. Do you place yours there? What about that bird insisting that it's spring despite the snow? She's awfully sure, now, isn't she? Belief. Is it static? Once you've got it, does it remain certain as the sky above? Or can life experiences knock faith on its head?

Do you believe in the material world, what money can buy? A gleaming red car goes racing by, and as much as you love that machine, do you believe in it? Is it worthy of belief? The kiss is as invisible as air, yet you inhale its magic over and over again. Twenty years from now, will that kiss still make you swoon? Will it hold your faith? Could either of those things change your life? It can take time to know where your faith is best placed. Some things may hold your faith for your entire life. Others may shift, shuffling your belief like a deck of cards. Since faith isn't something you can hold in your hand, buy a candy bar with, or trade for a fine pair of shoes, is it unreal? You can't put it in the bank, drive it to Mexico, or break its back. Or can you?

What does faith ask of us? Al Young, in his poem "Faith," says, "Knowing knows it knows. . . . Faith trusts." Then faith holds a piece of the unknown, and to have it means you take the risk you might be wrong. But something more than just curiosity is holding your belief. Something along with doubt keeps you from being entirely certain. Might this be the mystery of life? Young goes on to say, "Faith knows how to imagine. . . ." And without that, where's life? Where's religion, science, the whole nine yards?

The Israeli poet Yehuda Amichai wrote, "From the place where we are right / flowers will never grow / in the spring." Faith leaves room for questions. When we insist we've got the answer, we become immobile, stuck in cement. Being right leaves no room for movement, no room for lightning to strike us awake and alive. Being right shuts off the possibility for "I don't know," which is pretty important if you're going to live alert to new information, new love, and a sunset so brilliant you've got to rub your eyes just to make sure it's real.

Who are the "believers"? Are you one? In her poem "Churchgoing," Marilyn Nelson says, "[S]ometimes it causes me to tremble, / that they believe most, who so much have lost." If we lose and lose again, then is belief all we can rely on, the maybe of it, the distant future of it? If we're lost, is belief all we have with which to fortify ourselves? Neglect or misfortune aren't always ingredients for belief, are they? Don't they grow disbelief as well? Linda Hogan writes, "I too have wanted to give up / on everything / when what was right turned wrong."

The poet Rumi, who lived in the thirteenth century, said, "It's better to hide completely within" when those around him were faithless. Where do you hide? Might you hide in a poem? Or do you not hide, but stand on a hilltop, proclaiming what you believe in the face of indifference or the stone throwers of doubt? What gives you that strength?

Doubt, that pesky, gnawing thing that bites at the heels, or worse, at the heart: Can you put a leash on it finally, or give it a bone? Or does doubt turn up its nose at that morsel and bark all night? In her poem "Doubt," Sara Holbrook writes, "It sure would be / a faster route, / if I could live / without a doubt." Doubt is real trouble when it eats us alive. And as it feasts, it gets bigger and bigger while the self grows tinier and tinier. If we can keep doubt outside, say, at jacket level rather than inside our skin, we're better off, most times.

But doesn't doubt serve us too, sometimes—doubt in ourselves and others? A niggling doubt in oneself can cause one to take a second look, think a little longer. Maybe those next thoughts will lead one to greater understanding. William Heyen's poem "The Berries" confronts doubt in a significant way. A Nazi commandant is playing cards with a Jewish woman prisoner who's about to be sent to the ovens. A little more doubt on his part about the coming action would have saved her life and possibly the lives of many others.

What happens when we're doubted, especially by someone we regard highly? In his poem "The Dog Who Walked on

Water," Elliot Ruchowitz-Roberts writes of watching a dog do the impossible. The dog kept walking on water until he saw the doubt on the faces of the people on shore, then lost something of his own possibility. It's one thing when your pup loses faith in his nascent self; it's another thing when your own trust is ripped out from under you. In "The Dirty Hand," Carlos Drummond de Andrade turns self-doubt into art. His loathing is so big, he says, "My hand is dirty. / I must cut it off." Might poetry help him get his faith back? Might it help him keep his "hand"?

Children know something about faith that many adults forget. Teenagers can straddle both the child and the adult world. One foot in imagination and trust and the other reaching toward the solid ground of reason. Don't hurry your step! Think of Charles Simic's poem "School for Visionaries": "Your invisible friend, what happened to her?" Do you remember yours? Or has she faded with the shoelaces you once couldn't tie and the street at which you waited for a hand to hold before crossing. Casper the Friendly Ghost and the Virgin Mary once shared my bed! We had long discussions before sleep came. When they left, where did they go? To another child, another willing believer, I hope. May Swenson writes of an experience of imaginary play. All day she's been in the field, riding her stick-horse. Although her mother questions her when she comes home, Swenson holds on to her imaginary world; that horse neighed and whinnied like any other.

When my husband was a boy, growing up in a Catholic, churchgoing family, there were some Sundays when his dad said, "We're going to have church at home today." His mother may have rolled her eyes, but the family went out into the backyard, and they celebrated the trees and the grass, and found God. In his poem "Bible," Joseph Stroud does this too, showing us the primacy of even nature's smallest creatures: "The spider crab exults: *Look at me! I, too, am of the glory of this world.*"

The Chilean poet Pablo Neruda writes, "Poetry arrived / in search of me. I don't know, I don't know where / it came from. . . ." What of this belief? What does it tell us about the world we live in? Neruda was called to write. Inspiration took hold and knocked him into its force field. It's as though poetry came from outside of him. It may be that the outside world—the people of Santiago or his rural hometown—brought him a sense of the world that was poetry. Perhaps the scents of the marketplace woke him up. Whatever the outside stimulus, something dormant inside Neruda was enlivened. His imagination was stirred. Some things we discover with a part of us that transcends reason and rational thinking. Imagination knows something logic forgets. To pay it any heed at all requires faith.

Life has sucked my belief out of many things. But in poetry, my faith remains mostly whole. Often my poems hide from me throughout a whole winter. They hang out below the ground, groveling with earthworms, but I can't believe that. My faith in writing falters, until spring calls it back. A bell in my heart rings, reminding me of poetry. No matter how a poem succeeds or doesn't in the larger world, that's not what my art thrives on. It lives for the words unbidden whispering in my ear, waking me at dawn, insisting that I rush rush, sleep-worn, to my desk to catch the poem before it flees like so many dreams. That means more to me than any external success—a fancy prize or a hefty check—ever could.

Writers are fueled by both faith and doubt, not necessarily in equal measure. Faith may get one to the page but it's doubt that holds one there. The desire to prove doubt wrong is compelling. You may get lost, but then you'll get found; the words will find you. It's the "I don't know" that keeps the poet on the edge of her seat, keeps her coming back for more. Will a next word come? Will it be the right one? Or will a next word not come and the inspiration for the poem, the whole constellation of love that's pushing it forward into the poet's mind, blow away like dust? Is there anything here really worth having faith in?

To be able to say "Here's that word-dazzled poem I stayed up all night for! It managed to escape my fears, though they threw their poison darts" is heaven. The next time a poem comes calling, it's the same thing all over again. The poet would feed his poem caviar, even if he couldn't afford it, if the poem asked. Anything. And if the poem fails, if it comes out like putty instead of poetry, then what of faith? It gets lost for a while, perhaps. Then time for more of it, that's all.

Writing calls for a quiet kind of faith, a belief in the mystery of one word finding another, that the what-you're-afraid-you-don't-have-words-for can truly be said. Joy Castro writes, "My sacred secrets: . . . the chest's softening / that comes with rain at dusk." Faith isn't a promise; it's a possibility. Faith isn't certainty; it's a desire to sink into the murky mess of life and find the words for it. Those who want only sure things and certificates to hang on the wall don't become poets.

The writer Anna Paganelli believes that all stories are faith.

She says that "if we tell stories truthfully, we change the direction of our own lives." To tell a story or write a poem truthfully doesn't always mean sticking to the hard facts; it means striving to get to the heart of the matter, the heart of *your* matter. When that poem that you were carrying around in your soul for days or years gets written down, your life is changed. You've made something. You've chosen which words are the best ones. You've said, "Yes, that's what I wanted to say." The words are held by the paper, so you don't have to crush them to your chest any longer. No one can say, "That's not right." (At least not yet.) The poem on the page gives you more to have faith in. Then the ground you stand on is a bit firmer. Your shoes take to the pavement with more pizzazz. Might those be sparks you leave in your wake? Or just poetry?

So, what will you believe? These poems are here for you to read and question, believe in and doubt, and hold up to the light. Hold them up to your doubt and see what happens. Measure them against your faith. The earliest poem in this collection comes from 600 B.C.E. The most recent one is merely a few months old. People have been grappling with questions of faith and doubt since the very beginning of time. You may find that your own questions lead you to paper and pencil too.

—Patrice Vecchione

GOD SAYS YES TO ME

I asked God if it was okay to be melodramatic
and she said yes
I asked her if it was okay to be short
and she said it sure is
I asked her if I could wear nail polish
or not wear nail polish
and she said honey
she calls me that sometimes
she said you can do just exactly
what you want to
Thanks God I said
And is it even okay if I don't paragraph
my letters
Sweetcakes God said
who knows where she picked that up
what I'm telling you is
Yes Yes Yes

Kaylin Haught

MY GRANDFATHER'S HAT

In my family we have similar hair.
My father's hair is a lot like mine,
dark blond with some curl.
My mother's hair is like my brother's,
straight, blond and lightened by the sun.

The only one with hair that is different
is my grandfather.
His hair is short and sticks out
like his moustache,
but is as soft as the down on a baby bird.
You can tell his hair was once black
but it now surrounds his head
like a thin cloud of white.

Although I know his hair well,
I'm better acquainted with his hat,
deep blue with a small bronze whale
pinned on the front
and a smell of its own,
not a bad smell, deep and rich.

Even at the hospital,
when my grandfather's hair
grew weak and thin, there was his hat.

Sometimes my brother would take his hat
and wear it while we sat next to his bed.
And while my father and mother talked endlessly
with the doctors and nurses,
we talked with my grandfather
and his hat.

When he got better, we would take walks
in the morning, and his hat was there,
protecting him from the cold
and bringing back his hair.

Sometimes this hat was replaced by another
like the bright, yellow rubber hat
he wore only in the rain
to wave us off to school.

Nicholas Gardner

THE GIRL WHO LOVED THE SKY

Outside the second grade room,
the jacaranda tree blossomed
into purple lanterns, the papery petals
drifted, darkening the windows.
Inside, the room smelled like glue.
The desks were made of yellowed wood,
the tops littered with eraser rubbings,
rulers, and big fat pencils.
Colored chalk meant special days.
The walls were covered with precise
bright tulips and charts with shiny stars
by certain names. There, I learned
how to make butter by shaking a jar
until the pale cream clotted
into one sweet mass. There, I learned
that numbers were fractious beasts
with dens like dim zeros. And there,
I met a blind girl who thought the sky
tasted like cold metal when it rained
and whose eyes were always covered
with the bruised petals of her lids.

She loved the formless sky, defined
only by sounds, or the cool umbrellas
of clouds. On hot, still days
we listened to the sky falling

like chalk dust. We heard the noon
whistle of the pig-mash factory,
smelled the sourness of home-bound men.

I had no father; she had no eyes;
we were best friends. The other girls
drew shaky hopscotch squares
on the dusty asphalt, talked about
pajama parties, weekend cookouts,
and parents who bought sleek-finned cars.
Alone, we sat in the canvas swings,
our shoes digging into the sand, then pushing,
until we flew high over their heads,
our hands streaked with red rust
from the chains that kept us safe.

I was born blind, she said, an act of nature.
Sure, I thought, like birds born
without wings, trees without roots.
I didn't understand. The day she moved
I saw the world clearly: the sky
backed away from me like a departing father.
I sat under the jacaranda, catching
the petals in my palm, enclosing them
until my fist was another lantern
hiding a small and bitter flame.

Anita Endrezze

NOT

In church, at home,
they fall about my head and shoulders,
pelting like hail, like spitballs, like stinging B-Bs:
the various, endless *thou-shalt-nots,*
a welter of prohibitions
of things unclean
or merely worldly,
things forbidden to us.
In my mother's voice, the preacher's voice,
the voice of Paul or Moses:
No.
So all right. I obey. My lips
stuck shut
with *seen-and-not-heard,*
glued tight
by fear of the rod not spared,
I shoulder the empty weight
of all God wants me
not to do.

My sacred secrets:
the arms' tender melt
when I carry my little brother,
the chest's softening
that comes with rain at dusk,

the eyes' following wonder
at the shining, twirling, unnamed flecks of dust
in a beam of light,
dancing, falling gold—
from dust I came, to dust will I return—
That endless feeling.
Holy of holies.

The grown-ups mention none of those.
I keep them to myself,
not quite, not
quite
comprehending
the genuine meaning of grace.

Joy Castro

THE CENTAUR

The summer that I was ten—
Can it be there was only one
summer that I was ten? It must

have been a long one then—
each day I'd go out to choose
a fresh horse from my stable

which was a willow grove
down by the old canal.
I'd go on my two bare feet.

But when, with my brother's jackknife,
I had cut me a long limber horse
with a good thick knob for a head,

and peeled him slick and clean
except a few leaves for the tail,
and cinched my brother's belt

around his head for a rein,
I'd straddle and canter him fast
up the grass bank to the path,

trot along in the lovely dust
that talcumed over his hoofs,
hiding my toes, and turning

his feet to swift half-moons.
The willow knob with the strap
jouncing between my thighs

was the pommel and yet the poll
of my nickering pony's head.
My head and my neck were mine,

yet they were shaped like a horse.
My hair flopped to the side
like the mane of a horse in the wind.

My forelock swung in my eyes,
my neck arched and I snorted.
I shied and skittered and reared,

stopped and raised my knees,
pawed at the ground and quivered.
My teeth bared as we wheeled

and swished through the dust again.
I was the horse and the rider,
and the leather I slapped to his rump

spanked my own behind.
Doubled, my two hoofs beat
a gallop along the bank,

the wind twanged in my mane,
my mouth squared to the bit.
And yet I sat on my steed

quiet, negligent riding,
my toes standing the stirrups,
my thighs hugging his ribs.

At a walk we drew up to the porch.
I tethered him to a paling.
Dismounting, I smoothed my skirt

and entered the dusky hall.
My feet on the clean linoleum
left ghostly toes in the hall.

Where have you been? said my mother.
Been riding, I said from the sink,
and filled me a glass of water.

What's that in your pocket? she said.
Just my knife. It weighted my pocket
and stretched my dress awry.

Go tie back your hair, said my mother,
and *Why is your mouth all green?*
Rob Roy, he pulled some clover
as we crossed the field, I told her.

May Swenson

FAITH

Like a clear stream that forever runs,
like the highway, freeways, main arteries,
which are in truth rivers, faith flows.
What's there to think about? Click.
At the flip of a switch, the tap of a button,
lights come on, whole global engines gyrate
almost noiselessly; electrons move and point
in perfectly correct directions—faith.

Mash on a floor and there's the rug, the earth,
that rolling river again underneath, intimate
as blood, which flows as breath, which flows,
as everything alive must ebb and flow.
Whom should we think the flowing has to stop?
Knowing knows it knows. Or better: Faith trusts
and needs itself more than anything faith thinks
it needs to believe to stay alive.

But when faith thinks or, worse, when faith explains,
watch out. To move out of the rain, but run
heels over head into the sea—what is the point?
To know exactly when to fall asleep
without a single hint from anyone—faith.
If that's the way it works, it works.
With living surety, time moves in time

and out of time through time zones so fluently
we barely know to catch more than a moment.

Faith knows how to imagine what's timeless
by what is timed. Faith carries the sun
inside itself and shines it out in the dark.

Al Young

SCHOOL FOR VISIONARIES

The teacher sits with eyes closed.
When you play chess alone it's always your move.
I'm in the last row with a firefly in the palm of my hand.
The girl with red braids, who saw the girl with red braids?

~~~

Do you believe in something truer than truth?
Do you prick your ears even when you know damn well
    no one is coming?
Does that explain the lines on your forehead?
Your invisible friend, what happened to her?

~~~

The rushing wind slides to a stop to listen.
The prisoner opens the thick dictionary lying on his knees.
The floor is cold and his feet are bare.
A chew-toy of the gods, is that him?

~~~

Do you stare and stare at every black windowpane
As if it were a photo of your unsmiling parents?
Are you homesick for the house of cards?
The sad late-night cough, is it yours?

Charles Simic

THE DOG WHO WALKED ON WATER
for Winnie

And [Jesus] said, Come. And when Peter was come down out of the ship,
he walked on the water, to go to Jesus.

But when he saw the wind boisterous, he was afraid; and beginning to
sink, he cried, saying, Lord, save me.

And immediately Jesus stretched forth *his* hand, and caught him, and
said unto him, O thou of little faith, wherefore didst thou doubt?

—Matthew 14:29–31

Geese afloat, mallards adrift, pelicans awaft, gulls
        supernatant,
effortlessly, ghostly, like Jesus walking on water,
and you, at the edge of the lake,
drawn by this miracle of buoyancy,
barked and bounded not so much after as towards them,
leaving solid land for onetwothreefoursteps—

        you were walking on water!

Then, to our boisterous screams of disbelief,
you stopped, hesitant, turned your head towards us, saw
our lack of faith, and, with your whiskered face
now puzzled and fearful,
sank into the murky waters
which did not part for but covered you.

Before we could even think to reach out our hands,
you had gasped to the surface,
now like any normal dog,
dog-paddling and panting your way
furiously towards shore, where,
once on solid ground,
with a shake of your tiny, baptized body,
like a priest anointing his flock of little faith,
you rebuked us with holy water
and made believers of us all.

Elliot Ruchowitz-Roberts

ECHOES

Mother and father knew God and were glad to explain.
I was happy to listen. Love is a conversation.
When I said yes, they agreed, and I agreed.

They touched me when they said. I understood
the touch before the words. There is nothing to argue
in being held closest. Had God been a lion,

I would have done my best to grow a mane,
and to catch lambs to leave dead on His doorstep.
I could catch nothing. I was left to believe.

Love echoes love. I said what I was told
for my pleasure in who told it, for my need
to be held in the telling, apart from true and false.

The conversation is over. Given a choice
between Dante and a stone over two graves,
what shall I read? I have no mother and father.

They have no God unless I remember one
as part of a conversation I forget
except that it pleased me to be touched in the telling.

John Ciardi

THE DEATH OF SANTA CLAUS

He's had chest pains for weeks,
but doctors don't make house
calls to the North Pole,

he's let his Blue Cross lapse,
blood tests make him faint,
hospital gowns always flap

open, waiting rooms upset
his stomach, and it's only
indigestion anyway, he thinks,

until, feeding the reindeer,
he feels as if a monster fist
has grabbed his heart and won't

stop squeezing. He can't
breathe, and the beautiful white
world he loves goes black,

and he drops on his jelly belly
in the snow and Mrs. Claus
tears out of the toy factory

wailing, and the elves wring
their little hands, and Rudolph's
nose blinks like a sad ambulance

light, and in a tract house
in Houston, Texas, I'm 8,
telling my mom that stupid

kids at school say Santa's a big
fake, and she sits with me
on our purple-flowered couch,

and takes my hand, tears
in her throat, the terrible
news rising in her eyes.

Charles Harper Webb

"FOR A WHILE WE LIVED WITH PEOPLE"

For a while we lived with people,
but we saw no sign in them of the faithfulness we wanted.
It's better to hide completely within
as water hides in metal, as fire hides in a rock.

Rumi

translated from the Persian by Coleman Barks

"THERE'S A STRANGE FRENZY IN MY HEAD"

There's a strange frenzy in my head,
of birds flying,
each particle circulating on its own.
Is the one I love *every*where?

Rumi

translated from the Persian by Coleman Barks

THE FAITHFUL

He thought about the child addicted to
cocaine at birth, the spasms of withdrawal
that wracked her, and how, when her father, who
doted on her, was shot in the head, a pool
of blood for their bed, she, just two years old,
brought him milk and slept with him and spread
a blanket over him to keep him warm.
He thought about the eighty-year-old woman

who went on with life while caring for her dead
sisters. She thought they were asleep, she told
police when neighbors called about the odor.
And then she wept, and showed them to the door.
He thought about the God who made this world.
The ways He moved. The faithful whom He called.

Ronald Wallace

DOUBT

Insecure
is a lace
untied
that in a race
trips me inside.

It hints
that I don't
have the stuff,
why try,
when I'm not good enough.
And once
I stumble
in my mind,
it's harder
not to fall behind.

It sure would be
a faster route,
if I could live
without a doubt.

Sara Holbrook

DOUBT

Who but has seen
Once in his life, when youth and health ran high,
The fair, clear face of truth
  Grow dark to his eye?
  Who but has known
Cold mists of doubt and icy questionings
Creep round him like a nightmare, blotting out
  The sight of better things.

A hopeless hour,
When all the voices of the soul are dumb,
When o'er the tossing seas
  No light may come,
  When God and right
Are gone, and seated on the empty throne
Are dull philosophies and words of wind,
  Making His praise their own.

Better than this,
The burning sins of youth, the old man's greed,
Than thus to live inane;
  To sit and read,
  And with blind brain
Daily to treasure up a deadly doubt,
And live a life from which the light has fled,
  And faith's pure fire gone out.

Until at last,
For some blest souls, but never here for all,
Burns out a sudden light,
    And breaks the thrall,
    And doubt has fled,
And the soul rises, with a clearer sight
For this its pain, its sorrow, its despair,
    To God and truth and right.

    Plead we for those
Gently and humbly, as befitteth men
On whom the same chill shade
    Broods now as then.
    So shall they learn
How an eternal wisdom rules above,
And all the cords of Being are bound fast
    To an unfailing love.

Sir Lewis Morris

SON OF THE COMMANDMENT
Chicago

"So, twelve years old! Soon you'll be *bar mitzvah,*
     a *mensch,* a human being. Yes, son,
a human being, you. 'Today I am a man,' you'll say,
like I did. Let's see what you know:
The serpent in the Bible, what language does he speak?

"What's wrong with you? He speaks Hebrew. Same as God.
Same as Abraham and Isaac.
Same as Jesus.
Who else speaks Hebrew?

"Adam and Eve. Noah, too, and the animals:
the giraffe, the kangaroo, the lion.
          Hebrew.
                    Hebrew.
Soon you'll speak Hebrew.
Yes, and you'll read it too. *Apostate!*

"You're going to Hebrew School.

"Why? So you can speak to God in His own language.
Lesson One: *Bar* means son, *mitzvah* means commandment.
Bar mitzvah: Son of the commandment.
Commandment, *mitzvah*: What God gave to Moses.

"Lesson Two: When did Jews get souls?

"Souls they got when they got *Torah*.
Torah. *Torah* is Commandments.
Torah is soul.

"So learn, *bar mitzvah* boy! Read. Learn the blessing.
Do it right and you'll see
          the letters fly up to heaven.

"Learn. Yes. There's money
                    in puberty,
          money in learning. Books, money, fountain
pens . . . Always remember: learning is the best merchandise.

"Lesson Three: *Daven* means pray. You rock back and forth
          like the rabbi,
                    and pray. In Hebrew.
From your mouth to God's ear.
But it has to be in Hebrew.
And you can't mispronounce:
And no vowels to make it easy."

Robert Sward

CHURCHGOING

after Philip Larkin

The Lutherans sit stolidly in rows;
only their children feel the holy ghost
that makes them jerk and bobble and almost
destroys the pious atmosphere for those
whose reverence bows their backs as if in work.
The congregation sits, or stands to sing,
or chants the dusty creeds automaton.
Their voices drone like engines, on and on,
and they remain untouched by everything:
confession, praise, or likewise, giving thanks.
The organ that they saved years to afford
repeats the Sunday rhythms song by song;
slow lips recite the credo, smother yawns,
and ask forgiveness for being so bored.

I, too, am wavering on the edge of sleep,
and ask myself again why I have come
to probe the ruins of this dying cult.
I come bearing the cancer of my doubt
as superstitious suffering women come
to touch the magic hem of a saint's robe.

Yet this has served two centuries of men
as more than superstitious cant; they died

believing simply. Women, satisfied
that this was truth, were racked and burned with them
for empty words we moderns merely chant.

We sing a spiritual as the last song,
and we are moved by a peculiar grace
that settles a new aura on the place.
This simple melody, though sung all wrong,
captures exactly what I think is faith.
Were you there when they crucified my Lord?
That slaves should suffer in his agony!
That Christian, slave-owning hypocrisy
nevertheless was by these slaves ignored
as they pitied the poor body of Christ!
Oh, sometimes it causes me to tremble,
that they believe most, who so much have lost.
To be a Christian, one must bear a cross.
I think belief is given to the simple
as recompense for what they do not know.

I sit alone, tormented in my heart
by fighting angels, one group black, one white.
The victory is uncertain, but tonight
I'll lie awake again, and try to start
finding the black way back to what we've lost.

Marilyn Nelson

"MY WORTHINESS IS ALL MY DOUBT"

My Worthiness is all my Doubt—
His Merit—all my fear—
Contrasting which, my quality
Do lowlier—appear—

Lest I should insufficient prove
For His beloved Need—
The Chiefest Apprehension
Upon my thronging Mind—

'Tis true—that Deity to stoop
Inherently incline—
For nothing higher than Itself
Itself can rest upon—

So I—the undivine abode
Of His Elect Content—
Conform my Soul—as 'twere a Church,
Unto Her Sacrament—

Emily Dickinson

YET DO I MARVEL

I doubt not God is good, well-meaning, kind,
And did He stoop to quibble could tell why
The little buried mole continues blind,
Why flesh that mirrors Him must some day die,
Make plain the reason tortured Tantalus
Is baited by the fickle fruit, declare
If merely brute caprice dooms Sisyphus
To struggle up a never-ending stair.
Inscrutable His ways are, and immune
To catechism by a mind too strewn
With petty cares to slightly understand
What awful brain compels His awful hand.
Yet do I marvel at this curious thing:
To make a poet black, and bid him sing!

Countee Cullen

LONG DROP TO BLACK WATER

What confidence led us into a rainy Ithaca night
neither I nor my friend knew. Swollen gorges
to our left, the ground crumbling
as we clung to tree trunks and hooked our fingers
into the tight loops of a gun factory fence,
sleighting a path in spray and fog
that swallowed our legs below the knees,
not knowing till the next day's retracking
how often we had hung, far from the eroded bank,
above nothing but a long drop to black water.

Whatever that confidence was, I've lost it.
But it informs the toads,
crouches them in crooked caves of alder roots,
pulses the pale skin under their slack mouths,
keeps them in the pond's tight waves clutching anything:
a pine's resinous knot, a fist of chair foam,
even a drowned and legless female.

Now in the sun's last light, unctuous through haze
that lifts the land above itself
and leans the alders over water in green flames,
I see more in the pasture's stubbed grass,
leaping sure and unwavering to the cold,
without thought of the ducks scouring the pond's edge

for the mass of eggs
or the snapper hungry on the gelid bottom.
What could bring them year after year
and always less in number
but faith in their own wholeness and desire.
Faith that I lack, faith that I want
in this spring, fecund and feral.

Judy Jordan

BARE-ROOT

I planted the apricot
near an old peach
at the edge of this storm
that exhausts a worn month
place the roots
into the earth just so
as if each had a predestined place
a warm sleeve in the soil

To allay these fears
that crowd close
in this dark
I revere now at all cost
the slow desperate days
toward spring
that pull hope
out of the bark

Stephen Meadows

"DOUBT THOU THE STARS ARE FIRE"

Doubt thou the stars are fire;
Doubt that the sun doth move;
Doubt truth to be a liar;
But never doubt I love.

William Shakespeare

THE SONG OF CHANG-GAN:
A STORY OF YOUNG LOVE

Bangs just beginning to cover my forehead,
I play, picking flowers near the front door.
You come by circling the well,
riding a bamboo horse, tossing green plums.
Together we live in the village of Chang-gan,
two children without doubt or dislike.

At fourteen I become your wife.
Bashful, I can't meet your gaze
but lower my head, look toward the dark wall.
Though you call a thousand times,
not once do I look up.

By fifteen my brows begin to ease.
Trusting our love, I want to be with you
till dust and ash. I don't think I'll have to climb
the lookout to watch for you.

At sixteen you travel far
through the dangerous gorge of Qu-tang,
the rapids hazardous and impassable come May.
Gibbons fill the air with their mournful calls.

When you left our gate you dragged your feet.
Now in each of your old steps

new moss grows, so deep, so thick,
impossible for me to sweep away.
The wind comes early and leaves fall.

Now it is Autumn. Past the west garden
the yellow butterflies swoop in pairs
I break at seeing them.
Color drains from my face;
I fear my youth is wasting.

If one of these days you will return
through the three gorges of the Yang-zi-jiang
send a letter home, and I will come to meet you,
no matter how far.

Li Po

translated from the Chinese by Alice Tao and Patrice Vecchione

WHAT SHOULD I SAY

What should I say,
   Since faith is dead,
And truth away
   From you is fled?
   Should I be led
   With doubleness?
   Nay, nay, mistress!

I promised you,
   And you promised me,
To be as true
   As I would be.
   But since I see
   Your double heart,
   Farewell my part!

Though for to take
   It is not my mind,
But to forsake
   [One so unkind]
   And as I find,
   So will I trust:
   Farewell, unjust!

Can ye say nay?
   But you said

Faith Doubt

Pages - 48

That I alway
   Should be obeyed?
   And thus betrayed
   Or that I wiste—
      Farewell, unkissed.

Sir Thomas Wyatt

BIBLE

The spider crab exults: *Look at me! I, too, am of the glory
of this world.* A field mouse turns to the snake: *This
is my body. This is my blood.* The scorpion scuttling
from under a rock, arms wide, pincers open, wants
to embrace us—it has news, friends—the tip
of its tail bears a psalm from Isaiah. And the heron
is Lord of the Apocalypse stalking across the pool,
choosing and stabbing: *This one. That one.
My chosen ones.*

Joseph Stroud

DOUBT

They bade me cast the thing away,
They pointed to my hands all bleeding,
They listened not to all my pleading;
The thing I meant I could not say;
I knew that I should rue the day
If once I cast that thing away.

I grasped it firm, and bore the pain;
The thorny husks I stripped and scattered;
If I could reach its heart, what mattered
If other men saw not my gain,
Or even if I should be slain?
I knew the risks; I chose the pain.

O, had I cast that thing away,
I had not found what most I cherish,
A faith without which I should perish,—
The faith which, like a kernel, lay
Hid in the husks which on that day
My instinct would not throw away!

Helen Hunt Jackson

THE GIRL AT FIVE

You hate a girl who has been molested.
You look at me with repulsion in your eyes
before turning away in disgust and loathing.

In the fresh morning air, I walked out the back door,
past the small garden, into the coolness of the garage.
He was waiting for me.

"It's not you," you say.

He was a man I had always known.
His skin olive, his hair dark,
like all the men in my family.

"But the way you cower and hide."

Moving quietly behind me, his body
closed off the light from the doorway.
I looked toward the old workbench
where the jar of marbles lived.

"The way you drain
the life out of anyone who tries to care for you."

He spoke to me; I did not turn.
This was before I looked grown-ups in the eye.

He put his hand on my shoulder.
I froze.
I was five years old that day.

"It's how you are angry
at the world, how you
are always the victim."

He slid his hand down my cheek,
touching my nose, cupping my chin.
My mind tuned only to the suck of his breath,
the heat of his body.
Every molecule of me tensed.

"It's not you,
but how you refuse to grow up, to stop
blaming everyone else, to stop whining,
crying, sneaking, lying.
It's how you look at me with so much
hunger in your eyes."

All that he wanted.
My body no longer my own.

Anna Paganelli

THE DIRTY HAND

My hand is dirty.
I must cut it off.
To wash it is pointless.
The water is putrid.
The soap is bad.
It won't lather.
The hand is dirty.
It's been dirty for years.

I used to keep it
out of sight,
in my pants pocket.
No one suspected a thing.
People came up to me,
wanting to shake hands.
I would refuse.
And the hidden hand
would leave its imprint
on my thigh.
And I saw
it was the same
if I used it or not.
Disgust was the same.

How many nights
in the depths of the house

I washed that hand,
scrubbed it, polished it,
dreamed it would turn
to diamond or crystal
or even, at last,
into a plain white hand,
the clean hand of a man,
that you could shake,
or kiss, or hold
in one of those moments
when two people confess
without saying a word . . .
Only to have
the incurable hand
open its dirty fingers.

And the dirt was vile.
It was not mud or soot
or the caked filth
of an old scab
or the sweat
of a laborer's shirt.
It was a sad dirt
made of sickness
and human anguish.
It was not black;
black is pure.
It was dull,
a dull grayish dirt.
It is impossible
to live with this

gross hand that lies
on the table.
Quick! Cut it off!
Chop it to pieces
and throw it
into the ocean.
With time, with hope
and its intricate workings
another hand will come,
pure, transparent as glass,
and fasten itself to my arm.

Carlos Drummond de Andrade

translated from the Portuguese by Mark Strand

OF THE TERRIBLE DOUBT OF APPEARANCES

Of the terrible doubt of appearances,
Of the uncertainty after all, that we may be deluded,
That may-be reliance and hope are but speculations after all,
That may-be identity beyond the grave is a beautiful
      fable only,
May-be the things I perceive, the animals, plants, men, hills,
      shining and flowing waters,
The skies of day and night, colors, densities, forms, may-be
      these are (as doubtless they are) only apparitions, and
      the real something has yet to be known,
(How often they dart out of themselves as if to confound me
      and mock me!
How often I think neither I know, nor any man knows,
      aught of them.)
May-be seeming to me what they are (as doubtless they
      indeed but seem) as from my present point of view, and
      might prove (as of course they would) nought of what
      they appear, or nought anyhow, from entirely changed
      points of view;
To me these and the like of these are curiously answer'd by
      my lovers, my dear friends,
When he whom I love travels with me or sits a long while
      holding me by the hand,
When the subtle air, the impalpable, the sense that words
      and reason hold not, surround us and pervade us,

Then I am charged with untold and untellable wisdom, I am
     silent, I require nothing further,
I cannot answer the question of appearances or that of
     identity beyond the grave,
But I walk or sit indifferent, I am satisfied,
He ahold of my hand has completely satisfied me.

Walt Whitman

NO DOUBT

He's your friend, he says. Of that there's no doubt.
He adores your roast boar, mullet, trout,
hare, chicken, sow's breast, oysters,
salmon and your famous wine.
If my dinners were as good as yours
he'd be a friend of mine.

Martial

translated from the Latin by Brendan Kennelly

LAST APPLE

"I am like the last apple
That falls from the tree
and no one picks up."
I kneel to the fragrance
of the last apple,
and I pick it up.

In my hands—the tree,
in my hands—the leaf,
in my hands—the blossom,
and in my hands—the earth
that kisses the apple
that no one picks up.

Malka Heifetz Tussman

translated from the Yiddish by Marcia Falk

YOU MAY FORGET BUT

Let me tell you
this: someone in
some future time
will think of us

Sappho

translated from the Greek by Mary Barnard

"EVERY WORD IS A DOUBT"

Every word is a doubt,
every silence another doubt.
However,
the intertwining of both
lets us breathe.

All sleeping is a sinking down,
all waking another sinking.
However,
the intertwining of both
lets us rise up again.

All life is a form of vanishing,
all death another form.
However,
the intertwining of both
lets us be a sign in the void.

Roberto Juarroz

translated from the Spanish by Mary Crow

THE DOUBT OF FUTURE FOES

The doubt of future foes exiles my present joy,
And wit me warns to shun such snares as threaten mine
    annoy;
For falsehood now doth flow, and subjects' faith doth ebb,
Which should not be if reason ruled or wisdom weaved
    the web.
But clouds of joys untried do cloak aspiring minds,
Which turn to rain of late repent by changèd course of
    winds.
The top of hope supposed the root upreared shall be,
And fruitless all their grafted guile, as shortly ye shall see.
The dazzled eyes with pride, which great ambition blinds,
Shall be unsealed by worthy wights whose foresight
    falsehood finds.
The daughter of debate that discord aye doth sow
Shall reap no gain where former rule still peace hath taught
    to know.
No foreign banished wight shall anchor in this port;
Our realm brooks not seditious sects, let them elsewhere
    resort.
My rusty sword through rest shall first his edge employ
To poll their tops that seek such change or gape for
    future joy.

Elizabeth I

WATCH GOD CRUMBLE

Bye bye, my man, goodbye

The first thing is
he didn't know
what I was doing

He had super 20/10 vision
but couldn't keep his eye
on me
the other birds
and the main chance, too

I was steady growing
finding the divine within myself
seeing what could happen
if I placed my faith
in me

I stopped saying my prayers
every night and every morning
stopped checking in each day
to learn
if the sky would fall
or whether the sun
was going to shine
in my backyard

Looked out the door
or the nearest window
for myself—
and he must have thought
I had gotten a bit too busy
or was trying to save money
on the phone bill
for a while

I had found an obeah woman
took three balm baths
and nobody was punishing me
for my heathenish sin
The devil hadn't signed my name
in his little black book

I no longer looked forward
to visitations of the spirit,
actually stopped asking him
for anything
He must have thought that meant
I needed nothing,
which had always been
the easiest thing he had
to give

Meanwhile, I was off
in greener pastures
restoring my own soul

I threw away my bride ring
all the beads
put sea salt in the holy water
and washed my hair
Then I tore up his special raiments
the robe he had blessed
and started using
the scraps from them
for dusting cloths

And he didn't seem to notice
when the energy changed
His magic wand,
that marvelous staff of life,
became just a well-grown stick
The fish was fried
too dry
the bread tasted stale
the red wine didn't go well
with the rest
of the evening meal

Maybe he had gotten
tired of listening
and thought I would always be there
humming

on the line,
stopped tuning in
didn't hear the static
until the phone cut off

By which time
I was dancing
to another music,
had flung my last two veils
away,
had figured out
that, okay,
he may have been
a real tough cookie
during his prime,
but in the end
he was just
another man

Akasha Gloria Hull

THE BERRIES

Translucent red berries shine
from honeysuckle branches rising
above my windowsill. I'm reading
of a camp commandant playing
cards with Jewish women
before sending them to the gas van.
I picture him just whiling away the time,
until it's time.

This spring again, everything is in memoriam,
berries are drops of lungblood
floating in the breath of one
who was and/or wasn't there with them,
their God. One woman holds
a winning hand, we see her grimacing
up at him, at Him. Everything
hovers in place. I keep reading,

the commandant hears the distinctive rumbling
of the idling truck, & checks his watch.
He's enjoyed them, these women. *Schade,* it's a pity
he'll need to break in new ones,

most of whom won't know the game or be
competent, in their own turn,
to shuffle, to deal. He returns her smile.
He checks his watch again.

William Heyen

DEAR NEIGHBOR GOD

Dear neighbor God, if sometimes I disturb
you in the middle of the night with my knocking,
it's because so often I can't hear you breathing
and know: you're alone over there.
And if you need something, and no one's there
to fill the cup and put it in your fingers,
I'm always listening. Only say the word.
I'm right here.
Only a little wall stands between us,
built by chance: for this is all it might take—
one cry from your mouth or mine,
and it would break down
and not make a scene, or sound.

It is made up of all your images.

And your images stand around you like names.
And if just once the light in me burns high
that shows the way to you from deep inside,
it goes to waste as glare spilling on their frames.

And my mind, so soon to stumble and go lame,
wanders away from you, homeless, exiled.

Rainer Maria Rilke

translated from the German by Steven Lautermilch

THE PLACE WHERE WE ARE RIGHT

From the place where we are right
flowers will never grow
in the spring.

The place where we are right
is hard and trampled
like a yard.

But doubts and loves
dig up the world
like a mole, a plow.
And a whisper will be heard in the place
where the ruined
house once stood.

Yehuda Amichai

translated from the Hebrew by Chana Bloch and Stephen Mitchell

PRAISE SONG

to my aunt blanche
who rolled from grass to driveway
into the street one sunday morning.
i was ten.   i had never seen
a human woman hurl her basketball
of a body into the traffic of the world.
Praise to the drivers who stopped in time.
Praise to the faith with which she rose
after some moments then slowly walked
sighing back to her family.
Praise to the arms which understood
little or nothing of what it meant
but welcomed her in without judgment,
accepting it all like children might,
like God.

Lucille Clifton

POETRY

And it was at that age . . . Poetry arrived
in search of me. I don't know, I don't know where
it came from, from winter or a river.
I don't know how or when,
no, they were not voices, they were not
words, nor silence,
but from a street I was summoned,
from the branches of night,
abruptly from the others,
among violent fires
or returning alone,
there I was without a face
and it touched me.

I did not know what to say, my mouth
had no way
with names,
my eyes were blind,
and something started in my soul,
fever or forgotten wings,
and I made my own way,
deciphering
that fire,
and I wrote the first faint line,
faint, without substance, pure
nonsense,

pure wisdom
of someone who knows nothing,
and suddenly I saw
the heavens
unfastened
and open,
planets,
palpitating plantations,
shadow perforated,
riddled
with arrows, fire and flowers,
the winding night, the universe.

And I, infinitesimal being,
drunk with the great starry
void,
likeness, image of
mystery,
felt myself a pure part
of the abyss,
I wheeled with the stars,
my heart broke loose on the open sky.

Pablo Neruda

translated from the Spanish by Alistair Reid

FINDERS KEEPERS

Just what can be found with eyes open?
$10,000 in coins, anyway.
Enough to fill a few five-gallon jugs.

When his friend asked for a loan,
"Take this," said my father,
pointing to a bottle full
of the small money
other men leave behind.
A kind of faith in the possibility
a nickel has.

The wristwatch I wear daily
was left on a park bench
till my father came along.
Once, shortly after my mother left,
bills were due and Dad was down
to soda crackers and cigar butts.
In line to buy a cigar,
with his shoe,
he reached for a fifty.

Most people look in the wrong direction,
locating faith above them.
Pennies don't fall

from Heaven.
They're down below; more likely
to be found near sewer drains,
on the asphalt, beside dog droppings
and spent matches, worn shoes
even beggars leave behind.

Patrice Vecchione

THE WAKING

I wake to sleep, and take my waking slow.
I feel my fate in what I cannot fear.
I learn by going where I have to go.

We think by feeling. What is there to know?
I hear my being dance from ear to ear.
I wake to sleep, and take my waking slow.

Of those so close beside me, which are you?
God bless the Ground! I shall walk softly there,
And learn by going where I have to go.

Light takes the Tree; but who can tell us how?
The lowly worm climbs up a winding stair;
I wake to sleep, and take my waking slow.

Great Nature has another thing to do
To you and me; so take the lively air,
And, lovely, learn by going where to go.

This shaking keeps me steady. I should know.
What falls away is always. And is near.
I wake to sleep, and take my waking slow.
I learn by going where I have to go.

Theodore Roethke

ADVERTISEMENT

I'm a tranquillizer.
I'm effective at home.
I work in the office.
I can take exams
or the witness stand.
I mend broken cups with care.
All you have to do is take me,
let me melt beneath your tongue,
just gulp me
with a glass of water.

I know how to handle misfortune,
how to take bad news.
I can minimize injustice,
lighten up God's absence,
or pick the widow's veil that suits your face.
What are you waiting for—
have faith in my chemical compassion.

You're still a young man/woman.
It's not too late to learn how to unwind.
Who said
you have to take it on the chin?

Let me have your abyss.
I'll cushion it with sleep.

You'll thank me for giving you
four paws to fall on.

Sell me your soul.
There are no other takers.

There is no other devil anymore.

Wislawa Szymborska

translated from the Polish by Stanislaw Barańczak and Clare Cavanaugh

HOPE, FEAR, AND DOUBT

Such hope, as is the sick despair of good,
Such fear, as is the certainty of ill,
Such doubt, as is pale Expectation's food
Turned while she tastes to poison, when the will
Is powerless, and the spirit . . .

Percy Bysshe Shelley

IN THOSE DAYS

1.
On the first of May I entered Central Prison
and the Royal Officers registered me a communist.
I was tried, as was the custom then,
and my shirt was black with a yellow tie.
I left the hall followed by the soldiers'
blows and the derision of the judge. I had
a woman and a book of palm fronds. In it I read
the first names. I saw detention stations
filled with lice, others filled with sand,
others empty except of my face.
When we were thrown in the imprisonment that has yet
        to end,
I vowed: "This heart's yearning will not end."
You who will reach my kin, tell them it will not end.
Tonight we rest here, and in the morning we reach Baghdad.

2.
I celebrate this night with the moon visiting
from behind bars. The guard asleep, and the breathing
of Sibah is weighed with the humidity of the Shatt.
The visiting moon turns toward me. I am humming
in the corner of the holding station. What have you
        brought me
in your eyes? Air I can touch? Greetings from her?

The visiting moon enters through the bars and sits
on the corner of the station covered with my blanket.
He holds my palm. "You're lucky," he says
and leaves.
                    And in my hands I held
                                        a key made of silver.
All songs disappear except people's songs.
And if a voice can be bought, people will not buy it.
Willfully, I forget what is between people and me.
I am one of them, like them, and their voice retrieved.

3.
On the third of May I saw six walls crack.
A man I knew emerged through them, wearing
workers' clothes and a black leather cap.
I said: "I thought you left. Wasn't
your name among the first on the list?
Did you not volunteer in Madrid? Did you
not fight along the revolution's ramparts in Petrograd?
Weren't you killed in the oil strike?
Did I not see you in a papyrus thicket
loading your machine gun? Did you not raise
the commune's red flag? Did you not organize
the people's army in Sumatra?
Take my hand; the six walls may collapse
at any moment. Take my hand."

Neighbor, I believe in the strange star.
Neighbor, life's nights echo: "You are my home."
We've traveled wide and long

and the heart is still aimed at home.
Neighbor, don't stray.
My path leads to Baghdad.

Saadi Youssef

translated from the Arabic by Khaled Mattaw

LOVE'S DOUBT

'Tis love that blinds my heart and eyes,—
I sometimes say in doubting dreams,—
The face that near me perfect seems
Cold Memory paints in fainter dyes.

'Twas but love's dazzled eyes—I say—
That made her seem so strangely bright;
The face I worshipped yesternight,
I dread to meet it changed to-day.

As, when dies out some song's refrain,
And leaves your eyes in happy tears,
Awake the same fond idle fears,—
It cannot sound so sweet again.

You wait and say with vague annoy,
"It will not sound so sweet again,"
Until comes back the wild refrain
That floods your soul with treble joy.

So when I see my love again
Fades the unquiet doubt away,
While shines her beauty like the day
Over my happy heart and brain.

And in that face I see no more
The fancied faults I idly dreamed,
But all the charms that fairest seemed,
I find them, fairer than before.

John Milton Hay

THE DIRECTION OF LIGHT

New stones have risen up earth's labor
toward air. Everything rises,
the ocean in a cloud,
the rain forest passing
above our heads.
Children grow inch by inch
like trees in a graveyard,
victors over the same gravity
that pulls us down.
Even our light continues
on through the universe, and do we stop to
wonder who will see it
and where,
when the light of this earth is gone?
May there long be our light.

And then it falls. Shades are pulled down
between two worlds, clouds fall
as rain, light returns
the way rain from Brazil falls
in New York and the green parrots
in their cages feel it, shake their
feathers, and remember home
and are alive
and should they be thankful

for that gift
or should they curse like sailors and grieve?

I tell the parrots,
I too have wanted to give up
on everything
when what was right turned wrong
and the revolutionaries
who rose up
like yeast in life's bread, turned
against those who now rise up.

That's why I take the side of light—
don't you?—with the weight of living
tugging us down and earth wanting us back
despite great thoughts and smiling faces
that are prisons in between
the worlds of buying
and selling even the parrots
we teach to say "Hello."

Hello. Did I call this poem
the direction of light?
I meant *life*
so let this word
overthrow the first
and rise up to the start.

Linda Hogan

DIAMOND DARK

Wise folks always ask
   if a tree falls
in the forest does it
   make a sound?

But what I want to know is
   does a diamond buried
     deep in the earth
still shine?

The answer is the same
   I think
as how the dullest, darkest coal
   can turn into the most brilliant stone

It's the yes and no
   of things
How one holds
   the other

How one wholes
   the other
so that sound always becomes
    silence
   becomes sound

light always becomes
      darkness
   becomes light

Whether I'm there to see
   hear it
or not

Marilyn Singer

THE ATHEIST'S PRAYER

Hear my plea you, God who doesn't exist,
and in your nonexistence gather these, my grumblings.
You who never leave poor humans
without false comfort. You don't resist

our pleas and you disguise our desires.
The more you move yourself away from my mind,
the more I remember the calm fairy tales
my nursemaid told me to sweeten sad nights.

How vast you are, my God! You are so vast
that you are nothing but an Idea; reality is so narrow
however much it expands itself

to meet you. I suffer at your cost,
nonexistent God. For if you did exist
I too would truly exist.

Miguel de Unamuno
translated from the Spanish by Gaël Rozière and Patrice Vecchione

"WHEN I WAS FIVE"

When I was five, I knew God had made the world and everything in it. I knew God loved me, and I knew the dead were
in heaven with God always. I had a sweater. I draped it on a
fence, and when I turned to pick it up a minute later, it was
gone. That was the first time I had lost anything I really
loved. I walked in circles, too frightened to cry, searching for
it until dark. I knew my sweater was not in heaven, but if it
could disappear, just vanish without reason, then I could disappear, and God might lose me, no matter how good I was,
no matter how much I was loved. The buttons on my sweater
were translucent, a shimmering, pale opalescence. It was yellow.

Gary Young

WASTE

Not even waste
is inviolate.
The day misspent,
the love misplaced,
has inside it
the seed of redemption.
Nothing is exempt
from resurrection.
It is tiresome
how the grass
re-ripens, greening
all along the punched
and mucked horizon
once the bison
have moved on,
leaning into hunger
and hard luck.

Kay Ryan

A PRAYER TO THE NEW YEAR

In our hands is a fresh yearning for you,
in our eyes songs of praise and unique melodies,
into your hand as choral offerings we will thrust them.
O you who emerge as a sweet fountain of hope,
O you who are rich with promise and desire.
What is in store for us that you hold?
What have you got?

~~~

Give us love, for with love the treasures of bounty within us
burst forth . . .
With love our songs will grow green and will flower
and will spring with gifts
riches
fertility.

~~~

Give us love, so we may build the collapsed universe
        within us
anew
and restore
the joy of fertility to our barren world.

~~~

Give us wings to open the horizons of ascent,
to break free from our confined cavern, the solitude
    of iron walls.
Give us light, to pierce the deepest darkness
and with the strength of its brilliant flow
we will push our steps to a precipice
from which to reap life's victories.

Fadwa Tuqan

translated from the Arabic by Samira Kawar

LET EVENING COME

Let the light of late afternoon
shine through chinks in the barn, moving
up the bales as the sun moves down.

Let the cricket take up chafing
as a woman takes up her needles
and her yarn. Let evening come.

Let dew collect on the hoe abandoned
in long grass. Let the stars appear
and the moon disclose her silver horn.

Let the fox go back to its sandy den.
Let the wind die down. Let the shed
go black inside. Let evening come.

To the bottle in the ditch, to the scoop
in the oats, to air in the lung
let evening come.

Let it come, as it will, and don't
be afraid. God does not leave us
comfortless, so let evening come.

Jane Kenyon

Biographical Notes

The quotes contained within the biographies below are from interviews, letters, or readily available sources, such as the World Wide Web.

YEHUDA AMICHAI (1924–2000) is considered by many to be the greatest modern Israeli poet. Amichai was born in Germany, and with his family immigrated to Palestine in 1936. Raised speaking both German and Hebrew, he was one of the first to write in colloquial Hebrew. His poems, which often deal with the concerns of everyday life, are accessible, displaying gentle irony and expressing great love for people, his religion, and for the land of Israel, especially Jerusalem. He fought in World War II and in the Israeli War of Independence, and later became a believer in peace and reconciliation. He was actively involved with Palestinian writers. The recipient of many literary awards, Amichai was also nominated for the Nobel Prize for Literature. Amichai wrote, "Close one sad eye. Yes. Close the other sad eye. Yes. I can see now."

SELECTED READING
Open Closed Open: Poems (translated by Chana Bloch and Chana Kronfeld; Harcourt)
The Selected Poetry of Yehuda Amichai (translated by Chana Bloch and Stephen Mitchell; University of California Press)

CARLOS DRUMMOND DE ANDRADE (1902–1987) is Brazil's most influential poet of the twentieth century. He was born in a rural village; his parents were farmers who owned their own land. De Andrade became a pharmacist, but left medicine for poetry. For most of his life he was employed by the Brazilian government, becoming the director of history for the National Historical and Artistic Heritage Service. His early poetry is formal and satirical, but later, as part of the group the Brazilian Modernists, who were known for using informal speech and unconventional syntax in their poetry, de Andrade turned to free verse. He's best known for his poems to the working man, in which he voiced the frustration of immigrants, those living rurally and those bored by their urban middle-class lives. His work expresses particular concern for children and poor people. The author of over fifteen volumes of poetry, de Andrade said, "Easy to occupy a place in a telephone book. Difficult to occupy someone's heart, to know that you're really loved."

The American poet Elizabeth Bishop, who translated de Andrade said in an interview with the literary journal *Ploughshares,* "He's supposed to be very shy. I'm supposed to be very shy. We've met once—on the sidewalk at night. He had just come out of the same restaurant, and he kissed my hand politely when we were introduced."

SELECTED READING
Travelling in the Family: Selected Poems (edited by Thomas Colchie and Mark Strand; Ecco Press/HarperCollins)

JOY CASTRO was born in Miami in 1967. She is the author of a memoir, *The Truth Book.* Ms. Castro teaches creative writing and literature at Wabash College in Indiana and in the MFA program at Pine Manor College in Boston. Her critical and creative writing appears in national journals and anthologies. Ms. Castro makes her home with her husband and son in rural Indiana.

"For me," Castro says, "writing poetry is itself a kind of wrestling with faith and doubt. Doubt that I have anything worth sharing with others wrestles with my faith that when we risk digging down deeply and honestly into our own intimate and quirky experiences and reflections, we cannot fail to connect with others' own most private thoughts and feelings; and doubt that words can express what I long to say wrestles with my faith that the effort can lead me home."

SELECTED READING

The Truth Book: Escaping a Childhood of Abuse Among Jehovah's Witnesses (Arcade Publishing)

JOHN CIARDI (1916–1986) was born in Boston to Italian immigrants. His forty books include collections of poetry, children's books, and the popular *How Does a Poem Mean?*, a book that looks at poetry from the inside. His translation of Dante's *Divine Comedy* is one of the finest. Ciardi wrote what he called the "unimportant poem." He wrote about simple, everyday things like drinking a cup of coffee. A veteran of World War II, Ciardi also tackled difficult subjects such as war in his poems. He said, "You don't have to suffer to be a poet; adolescence is enough suffering for anyone."

In 1961 he left university teaching to focus his attention on writing. He traveled around the United States giving readings and talks about poetry. He was a commentator for National Public Radio and CBS. His career as a children's book writer began because he wanted to introduce his own kids to poetry.

In *How Does a Poem Mean?* Ciardi said, "Neither the deadness of bad poetry nor the liveliness of good poetry can be located exclusively in the way the poet uses words. Yet certainly whatever is most characteristic of a good poet must begin with a special sensitivity to language."

SELECTED READING

The Collected Poems of John Ciardi (edited by Edward M. Cifelli; University of Arkansas Press)

The Divine Comedy by Dante Alighieri (translator; NAL Trade)

How Does a Poem Mean? (essays; Houghton Mifflin)

LUCILLE CLIFTON's (b. 1936) biographer, Hilary Holladay, writes, "Lucille Clifton is among those time-traveling souls who Walt Whitman believed 'would look back on me because I looked forward to them.'" Clifton not only looks back, and she does that a lot in her poems; she looks forward, to us, her readers. At least that's how it feels when one takes a book of hers off the shelf, as if she's talking right to you. Her work has garnered much acclaim, including the National Book Award. She is a fellow of the American Academy of Arts and Sciences and was elected chancellor of the Academy of American Poets in 1999. She lives in Columbia, Maryland.

The poet Langston Hughes "discovered" Clifton, entering a poem of hers into a contest that she went on to win. Clifton, who began writing poems as a child, found it wasn't a matter of choice but something as natural as breathing. When asked how one learns to write, she responded that it's by paying attention, not only to oneself but also to the world. Her first book of poetry was published when she was thirty-nine. Before that she'd published picture books for children, including the very popular *Everett Anderson* series.

Her poems tackle big issues—love and loss, poverty, slavery, and physical abuse. She doesn't turn away from any subject. When interviewed on KCRW's *Bookworm,* Clifton said, "If you're going to tell a human story, you have to write about it all. It's very human to be angry, to be afraid."

SELECTED READING
Good Woman: Poems and a Memoir 1969–1980 (BOA Editions)
The Book of Light (poetry; BOA Editions)
Mercy (poetry; BOA Editions)
Wild Blessing, The Poetry of Lucille Clifton (by Hilary Holladay; Louisiana State University Press)

COUNTEE CULLEN (1903–1946) was a leading figure in the Harlem Renaissance, the African-American artistic movement of the 1920s that included other luminaries such as Langston Hughes and Zora Neale Hurston. Cullen believed that poetry didn't have a race, though he took the issue of race as a subject for poetry, such as the poem included here. Cullen was private about his life. What is known is that he was raised until the age of fifteen by a woman, not his mother, who brought him to Harlem. He was then unofficially adopted by a minister, whose last name Cullen took as his own. As a child he won a poetry contest and his poem was widely reprinted. In his early twenties Cullen's first book of poems was published. It included "Yet Do I Marvel." He received his master's degree from Harvard University. Before he was thirty he'd published four books, winning more recognition for poetry than any other black poet at that time. He received first prize in the Witter Bynner Foundation's poetry contest and a Guggenheim Fellowship. Cullen committed himself to promoting the work of other black writers. He taught at a junior high school in New York City, which may have taken his attention away from writing poetry and been the partial cause of the fall his reputation took in the late 1920s. His most famous student was James Baldwin.

Countee Cullen said, "If I am going to be a poet at all, I am going to be POET and not NEGRO POET. This is what has hindered the development of artists among us. . . . [W]hat I mean is this: I shall not write of negro subjects for the purpose of propaganda. That is not what a poet is concerned with. Of course, when the emotion rising out of the fact that I am a negro is strong, I express it."

SELECTED READING
My Soul's High Song (poetry and prose; Anchor)
On These I Stand: An Anthology of the Best Poems of Countee Cullen (Harper)

EMILY DICKINSON (1830–1886) wrote over 1,700 poems but during her lifetime published only seven of them. After her death her poems were found on scraps of paper; some she'd bound into booklets. Dickinson was creative in her use of punctuation, using dashes and unexpected capital letters. Sadly, when her poems were first published they were heavily edited, her unique punctuation replaced by standard forms. Dickinson's voice was a first; she was an original. Dickinson's great love for the natural world that she spent much time observing is evident in her poems. She truly wrote as she saw the world, producing poems that were completely unlike anything that was being written by her contemporaries or anything previously written. Though she led a quiet, cloistered life in her family's house in Amherst, Massachusetts, her mind was anything but confined. Dickinson's life was unconventional for her time. She never married and did not conform to a traditional religion. It's most doubtful that when Dickinson wrote "Fame is a fickle food upon a shifting plate," she had any idea she'd become one of the world's most favorite poets, though from that comment it is certain she knew about fame's pitfalls. Dickinson knew that writing could go beyond mere language and reason. She wrote, "[When] I feel physically as if the top of my head were taken off, I know that is poetry."

SELECTED READING

The Complete Poems of Emily Dickinson (edited by Thomas H. Johnson; Little, Brown)

The Life of Emily Dickinson (by Richard B. Sewall; Harvard University Press)

ELIZABETH I (1533–1603) was the daughter of Anne Boleyn and Henry VIII. She reigned as queen of England for forty-four years. The kingdom she inherited was one in turmoil. Much of the unrest was over religion. But she was a calm and calculating ruler who used her political savvy to great advantage. Persecution of Protestants forced her into a war she had tried to avoid. Her ability to compromise around religious issues made life easier. Known as the

Virgin Queen, her refusal to marry Philip II of Spain made the Spanish king so angry he sent his fierce army to raid England. The battle was easily won by the English. During her years in power literature blossomed, this being the time of Spenser, Marlowe, and Shakespeare. Expansion into the New World went forward. Queen Elizabeth I believed in education, thus it flourished during her reign. Her love of beautiful, ornate clothing also influenced the times. She came to be known as Good Queen Bess.

SELECTED READING
The Life of Elizabeth I (by Alison Weir; Ballantine Books)

Writer and artist **ANITA ENDREZZE** (b. 1952) is half Yaqui Indian and half Caucasian. Her most recent book *Throwing Fire at the Sun, Water at the Moon* is a tribal history told through myth, poetry, and story. Her book *at the helm of twilight* won both the Washington State Governor's Writers Award and the Seattle Bumbershoot/ Weyerhaeuser Award. Endrezze is currently at work on a novel about a vampire named Anton Jaeger. Her advice for young writers is "Write and write. Edit ruthlessly." She makes her home in Everett, Washington, with her family.

About "The Girl Who Loved the Sky," Endrezze writes that because of her parents' divorce when she was only six, uncommon at that time, and because of her ethnic background, "I felt apart from the rest of the kids. And I met a blind girl who was also 'different.'" The impact of that friendship inspired this poem.

SELECTED READING
Throwing Fire at the Sun, Water at the Moon (University of Arizona Press)

NICHOLAS GARDNER (b. 1990) lives in Santa Cruz, California. He resides in a mountain home with his parents, brother, and many domesticated creatures. Gardner says, "I wrote this poem about my grandfather, one of the most inspiring people in my life. His struggle with cancer marked many of my childhood years, and the fear of losing him, my best friend, left its mark on my heart."

KAYLIN HAUGHT (b. 1947) was born in Albion, Illinois, and raised on the Oklahoma prairie. Her father was a preacher and oil field worker, her mother a homemaker. Haught writes, "Poetry brings me closer to belief. Though 'God Says Yes' was written in a playful mood, it speaks of a connection I always feel, especially when out of doors. Like you and a deer, suddenly being made aware of each other in a clearing." Reminding us that there are many ways to go about being a writer, Haught says this about her writing life: "I've been writing pretty much in self-described and self-chosen obscurity for a long time. Over the years I've honed my craft and my mind in how it thinks and works. I'm just getting it out there!"

SELECTED READING
In the Palm of Your Hand: The Poet's Portable Workshop (by Steve Kowit; Tilbury House Publishers)

Lawyer and politician **JOHN MILTON HAY** (1838–1905) was a Secretary of State under President Lincoln. He traveled to Europe for the U.S. legation. Upon his return to the United States he became a journalist and wrote a major biography of Lincoln. Hay was an ambassador to Great Britain and later appointed Assistant Secretary of State. He was present in the theater when Lincoln was killed. Influential in creating the Open Door Policy with China, Hay also negotiated several treaties that were instrumental in preparations for usage of the Panama Canal. John Milton Hay said, "All who think cannot but see there is a sanction like that of religion which binds us in partnership in the serious work of the world."

SELECTED READING
John Milton Hay: The Union of Poetry and Politics (by Howard I. Kushner; Twayne Publishers)

WILLIAM HEYEN (b. 1940) was raised on Long Island by German immigrant parents. He received his Ph.D. from Ohio University, was a Senior Fulbright Lecturer in American Literature in Germany, and has received a Guggenheim Fellowship and awards from the National Endowment for the Arts and the American Academy of Arts and Letters, among others. His book *Crazy Horse in Stillness: Poems* won 1997's Small Press Book Award for Poetry, and *Shoah Train: Poems* was a finalist for the National Book Award in 2004.

William Heyen writes: "I no longer remember where I read—it was only a brief mention—of the concentration camp commandant who enjoyed playing cards with Jewish women before sending them to the gas van. Apparently, as I began to write his/His poem, I sensed a 'floating' and hovering evil even within the beauty of spring outside my window. As I wrote, my commandant became, as quiet as the poem is, as understated as it is, oblivious and banal, a kind of gregarious beast who, however inconvenient it is to him and his enjoyment, will be punctual in his contribution to the slaughter. And the particular victim here, the woman holding a winning hand, thinks whether she chooses to declare it or not will be important regarding her fate, but we know that hers is a choiceless Holocaust choice where all language is compromised, that she is doomed."

SELECTED READING
Confessions of Doc Williams and Other Poems (Etruscan Press)
Shoah Train: Poems (Etruscan Press)

Poet, fiction author, playwright, and essayist **LINDA HOGAN** (b. 1947) is a member of the Chickasaw people. The daughter of an army sergeant, she and her family moved frequently. Much of her childhood was spent in Oklahoma and Colorado. As a young woman she supported herself with odd jobs and as a freelance writer, before her success as an author gained her national recognition and she became an assistant professor at Colorado College. She now teaches American Indian studies at the University of Minnesota. Ms. Hogan's work expresses her relationship with the natural world, a traditional, indigenous, feminist perspective, and her love of the earth and commitment to its preservation. She has been active in the Native American movement. *Library Journal* refers to her work as "deep and full of grace" and says, "In Hogan's writing, the smallest detail can evoke a whole history."

In her book *Dwellings: A Spiritual History of the World,* Ms. Hogan writes that Native American elders believe "it is possible to wind a way backward to the start of things, and in so doing find a form of sacred reason, different from ordinary reason, that is linked to forces of nature."

SELECTED READING
The Book of Medicines (poetry; Coffee House Press)
Mean Spirit (novel; Ivy Books)
The Woman Who Watches Over the World: A Native Memoir (W. W. Norton)

Before becoming a full-time poet, **SARA HOLBROOK** (b. 1949), the author of many books of poetry for children, teens, and adults, went to school intending to go into journalism. She says, "I still think I write like a reporter. I gather gata from the world and sort of project myself into it. I write from the outside-in rather from the inside-out." Her book for teens *Walking on the Boundaries of Change* won the Parents' Choice Award. Holbrook holds writing workshops for students. She's the mother of two grown daughters and makes her home in Ohio with her Boston terrier, Mike. Holbrook says, "I started out writing poems for my children when they were little. The girls illustrated the poems, so it was a family thing."

SELECTED READING
Chicks Up Front: Poems (Cleveland State University Poetry Center)
I Never Said I Wasn't Difficult (poetry; Boyds Mills Press)
Walking on the Boundaries of Change (poetry; Boyds Mills Press)

AKASHA GLORIA HULL's (b. 1944) poems are featured in many anthologies and journals. Her first volume of poetry, *Healing Heart,* was published by Kitchen Table Press in 1989. Her latest book is *Soul Talk: The New Spirituality of African American Women.* Highlighting conversations with some of America's most influential black writers, *Soul Talk* is a blend of stories and practical advice about spirituality in daily life. Ms. Hull has received fellowships from the Rockefeller Foundation and the National Endowment for the Humanities, among others, and for many years was a professor of women's studies and literature at the University of California, Santa Cruz. About her poetry, writer Ntozake Shange said, "[W]e are blessed with another foreign tongue: the voice of a free, fearsome, sensual and vivid woman of color. Akasha Gloria Hull is 'family.' She's one of us. She means to live." An independent writer, professor, lecturer, and consultant, Ms. Hull is currently completing a novel.

In response to her poem "Watch god crumble," Hull writes, "I'm a very spiritual person who draws from many traditions and paths. At the end of a love affair which had soured, I found myself writing this irreverent, female rejection of a patriarchal god. I believe that the strongest faith emerges from doubt and questioning and must rest on firm, inner-self foundations which, paradoxically, that faith also helps to build."

SELECTED READING
Soul Talk: The New Spirituality of African American Women (Inner Traditions)

HELEN HUNT JACKSON's (1830–1885) best-known literary work is her historical romance novel *Ramona.* Jackson was born and raised in Amherst, Massachusetts, a schoolmate of Emily Dickinson. In 1879 she heard a lecture by Chief Standing Bear. He described how the Ponca Indians were forcibly removed from their homes on the Nebraska reservation. Jackson's fury at this treatment caused her to circulate petitions, raise money, and write letters in protest. Jackson was passionate and uncompromising about this cause. She turned her attention from writing to defending the rights of Native Americans. She worked especially on behalf of the Mission Indians of Southern California. Her book about the United States' Indian policy, *A Century of Dishonor,* was published in 1881. She sent a copy to every member of Congress, inscribing each book, "Look upon your hands; they are stained with the blood of your relations."

In describing writing her novel *Ramona,* which was often referred to as the "Uncle Tom's Cabin of California," Jackson said, "As soon as I began, it seemed impossible to write fast enough . . . I write faster than I would write a letter . . . two thousand to three thousand words in a morning, and I cannot help it."

SELECTED READING

A Century of Dishonor: A Sketch of the United States Government's Dealings with Some of the Indian Tribes (University of Oklahoma Press)

Ramona: A Story (Signet Classics)

Helen Hunt Jackson: A Literary Life (by Kate Phillips; University of California Press)

Poet and university professor **JUDY JORDAN**'s (b. 1961) first book of poetry won the 1999 Walt Whitman Award from the Academy of American Poets and the 2000 National Book Critics Circle Award. Her second collection of poems was recently published. She is currently working on a full-length play, a memoir, and a third book of poetry. Jordan built her own environmentally friendly Thoreau-like cabin with cordwood, and she hopes to build an earth-bag house. She devotes herself to animal rescue and is the founder of SIPRAW, which rescues dogs from puppy mills (www.sipraw.com). Jordan says, "I wrote 'Long Drop to Black Water' at a time in my life when I was deeply depressed. Even the process of writing is a life-affirming gesture and for me writing has been an act of self-love and healing. It was a long process to come to this realization, but I now realize that God loves me (whether I've earned it or not) and wants me to be creative. Thus for me, writing (no matter what the subject matter) is an act of faith and of thanking God for each day's opportunities and for my own abilities and talent."

SELECTED READING
Carolina Ghost Woods: Poems (Louisiana State University Press)
60¢ Coffee and a Quarter to Dance: A Poem (Louisiana State University Press)

The Argentine poet **ROBERTO JUARROZ** (1925–1995) was born in a small town near Buenos Aires. At eighteen he became a librarian, work he continued his whole life, later teaching library science. Juarroz was the author of fourteen collections of poetry. His first book was titled *Poesia Vertical,* "vertical poetry." His second book was called *Second Vertical Poetry,* the next *Third Vertical Poetry,* and so on. His are spare, compressed poems whose meanings are deeply felt. Juarroz's poetry has been compared to that of Rainer Maria Rilke and the author of the Tao Te Ching. In Argentina his poetry was acclaimed, but various political regimes disdained his work because of his contempt of politics, which he believed to be "whatever its color—the greatest adversary of poetry." American poet J. D. McClatchy said Juarroz's poems are "experience distilled to a crystaline drop of paradox." Juarroz translator Mary Crow is currently at work on a new translation of his poetry, entitled *Vertical Poetry: Last Poems.*

Poet, dramatist, and Martial translator **BRENDAN KENNELLY** (b. 1936) was a professor of modern literature at Trinity College in

Dublin for thirty years. He has published more than twenty poetry collections, most recently *Familiar Strangers: New & Selected Poems.* In his introduction to *Martial Art,* a collection of Martial's poetry, Kennelly writes, "Translation is a relationship. . . . This relationship is between two writers, two languages, and two times in time. Martial lived two thousand years ago. Today, he's alive and kicking."

SELECTED READING
Martial Art (translated by Brendan Kennelly; Bloodaxe Books)

JANE KENYON (1947–1995) grew up in the Midwest and received both a B.A. and an M.A. from the University of Michigan. She was the author of four books of poems, a book of translations of the poetry of Russian poet Anna Akhmatova, and a posthumously published collection of essays and interviews. Kenyon and her husband, Donald Hall, were the subjects of the Emmy Award–winning documentary *A Life Together.* Kenyon was the Poet Laureate of New Hampshire. She died of leukemia in 1995.

Her most lyrical poems are those in which she confronted her experience of depression and those in which she explored the nature of belief. In "With the Dog at Sunrise," Kenyon writes, "Searching for God is the first thing and the last, but in between such trouble, and such pain." In the essay "Thoughts on the Gifts of Art" from her book *A Hundred White Daffodils,* Kenyon wrote, "We cannot afford to ignore our inner lives, our imaginations, for when we do, we become capable of extreme cruelty and destruction."

SELECTED READING
Collected Poems (Graywolf Press)
A Hundred White Daffodils: Essays, Interviews, the Akhmatova Translations, Newspaper Columns, and One Poem (Graywolf Press)
Otherwise (poetry; Graywolf Press)

LI PO (c. 701–762) was born in western China, the son of a rich merchant, and grew up in Sichuan province. During his teens

Li Po learned swordsmanship and claimed to have killed several people in sword fights. His early poetry was favored by the court, and he received their patronage until he was exiled for an alliance with a rebellious member of the imperial family. Li Po spent many years traveling around China, joining a wandering band who called themselves "the Eight Immortals of the Wine Cup." Li Po lived during the Tang dynasty, a very accepting period in China's history. Literary life flourished.

Li Po believed in not losing a moment to enjoy his life, which included travel, wine, and love. A generous man, he gave away money to those in need, hard-luck scholars among them. Li Po's sense of self-importance and confidence were great, and he didn't hesitate to take sides politically.

Much of Li Po's poetry was written as ballads and songs. Some have compared his genius to that of Mozart. To this day he's considered China's most famous poet, "the Poet Immortal," known for his free spirit, wild imagination, and use of striking imagery, often based in the natural world. Chinese critics describe his writing as "a heavenly steed soaring across the air." Legend says Li Po died while trying to touch the moon's reflection in a lake. However, it's more likely he died from cirrhosis of the liver or from mercury poisoning from the containers that held the elixirs he drank in an attempt to promote longevity. Translator Alice Tao says, "Li Po was a man not afraid to be himself, even when arrogant. He was the Muhammad Ali of poetry—both confident men, both endowed with extraordinary talent. Despite their seemingly outrageous behavior, I am convinced they were just being themselves."

About the translation of "The Song of Chang-gan: A Story of Young Love," Patrice Vecchione writes, "Alice Tao and I wanted to capture the essence of the poem in a smooth, readable English and chose to omit the more obscure allusions and place names in an effort to make the poem accessible. First Alice, a native Chinese speaker, provided a direct, line-by-line translation of the poem, and I worked on finding the poetic language in English. We read many previous translations. Alice provided me with dictionary translations of specific words.

Many drafts of our translation came before we were happy with the one you read here. We wanted both meaning and rhythm to be right."

SELECTED READING
The Selected Poems of Li Po (translated by David Hinton; New Directions)

In about A.D. 40, the poet **MARCUS VALERIUS MARTIALIS** was born in Spain. There he received a traditional literary education. At twenty-five he traveled to Rome, where he lived for many years, meeting such writers as Lucan, Pliny the Younger, and Seneca. Some of these men introduced him to patrons who likely kept Martial from starvation. Martial's fame was based on a book of epigrams that he wrote sometime between the years 86 and 102. His poetry is a keen observation of all classes of the Roman people. Martial said, "It is feeling and force of imagination that makes us eloquent."

STEPHEN MEADOWS (b. 1949) is a Californian of Native American and pioneer descent. He holds a B.A. from the University of California, Santa Cruz, and a master's from San Francisco State University. One of his poems is featured on a bronze plaque in San Francisco. Meadows is a public radio broadcaster who has interviewed folk musicians from the United States, Canada, and the British Isles. About poetry Meadows says, "When, at times, all about one is desolation, always I return to the poems."

Welsh poet **SIR LEWIS MORRIS** (1833–1907) practiced law for many years before becoming a poet. He was knighted by Queen Victoria. It is likely his friendship with the controversial author Oscar Wilde prevented him from being named Poet Laureate. His poetry was noted for its metrical fluidity, which won him great popularity.

SELECTED READING
A Book of Verses (Lovell)

MARILYN NELSON (b. 1946) was born in Cleveland, Ohio, and began writing while in elementary school. Her work includes poetry not only for adults but also for young people and children. In 2001 her young adult biography in poetry about George Washington Carver was published to much acclaim. Nelson is the recipient of fellowships from the National Endowment for the Arts and the Fulbright, was a finalist in poetry for the National Book Award, and has received other significant recognition for her work. She comes from a long line of teachers on her mother's side and is a professor of English at the University of Connecticut and the Connecticut Poet Laureate. Ms. Nelson runs the Soul Mountain Retreat, a retreat for poets.

Ms. Nelson says, "The poem is in dialogue with Philip Larkin's earlier poem with the same title, and it was written during the period when I taught at St. Olaf College, a Norwegian Lutheran college in Northfield, Minnesota, as one of a handful of African Americans within a fifty mile vicinity. Everyone else was blond."

SELECTED READING
Carver: A Life in Poems (young adult biography; Front Street)
The Field of Praise (poetry; Louisiana State University Press)
A Wreath for Emmett Till (young adult poetry; Houghton Mifflin)

When he was only nineteen **PABLO NERUDA** (1904–1973) published his first collection of poems, beginning his long career as a poet. The following year he published *Twenty Love Poems and a Song of Despair,* one of his best known and most translated books, which caused a sensation because of its frank and intense expression of sexuality. Neruda was born in rural Chile. His father worked on the railroad and didn't take kindly to his son becoming a poet. In an effort to both respect and distance himself from his father he changed his name from Neftalí Ricardo Reyes Basoalto.

As a student Neruda lived in Santiago, struggling to find his way, driven by poetry and love. There's a story that one night Neruda went out dancing with a group of friends. When they arrived at the bar a man was bothering a woman on the dance floor, and skinny Neruda, dressed in his familiar black cape, intervened. Later, when Neruda and his friends were heading home, the man was waiting outside. Just as he was about to punch the young poet, he stopped, his fist an inch from Neruda's face, and said, "Aren't you Don Pablo?" The young poet said, "Yes." "*Perdóname!* I can't hit you. You are the reason my girlfriend loves me. I read her your poetry." At which point he brushed off Neruda's cape and sent the shaken poet on his way.

Neruda joined the Chilean diplomatic corps and worked in Burma, Java, and Singapore, where he led a lonely life and wrote poems. In his official capacity he went to Spain in 1935, a year before the outbreak of the Spanish Civil War. There he became friends with many poets, including Federico García Lorca. His public support of the Republican cause against the Fascist insurgents greatly embarrassed the Chilean government, and he was forced to resign. In 1939 Neruda was appointed consul for Spanish emigration in Paris, where he worked hard to make it possible for displaced Spaniards to immigrate to Chile. Neruda was active politically in Chile, serving as a senator, but had to flee the country when the government was taken over by right-wing extremists. In order to get out of Chile alive, he had to travel incognito. When he passed through the mountains on horseback, Neruda and his group stopped at a rural hot spring, where he was recognized and embraced as being a poet of the Chilean people. He later returned home to Chile when a new government came to power, and moved to a house on Isla Negra with the love of his life, Matilde Urrutia. By this time he was a national hero and an international celebrity.

Neruda received the Nobel Prize near the end of his life. His poetry totals over three thousand pages. Shortly after the murder of his friend Salvador Allende, Chile's president, during a right-wing coup, Neruda died. Though he was ill at the time, many Chileans believe he died of a broken heart, for the loss not only of Allende but also of his country. Following the coup a curfew was in place. On the day of Neruda's funeral thousands of people defied the orders to stay off the streets and joined the funeral procession as it made its way to the cemetery. Someone called out, "Salvador Allende?" And the group responded, "*Presente!*" Then the name of the famous musician also killed during the coup was called: "Victor Jara?" Again the crowd responded, "*Presente!*" And finally, "Pablo Neruda?" The swell of voices shouted, "*Presente!*" As certainly he was.

SELECTED READING

The Essential Neruda: Selected Poems (edited by Mark Eisner; City Lights Books)

Memoirs (translated by Hardie St. Martin; Farrar, Straus and Giroux)

Pablo Neruda: A Passion for Life (biography; by Adam Feinstein; Bloomsbury USA)

Twenty Love Poems and a Song of Despair (Penguin Books)

ANNA PAGANELLI (b. 1967) grew up in a suburb of San Francisco, where she spent her childhood wishing she lived someplace much more glamorous and exciting, such as New York City or perhaps the Taj Mahal. She's had many jobs, her most memorable being the one in which she climbed on top of huge houses and knocked down their chimneys with a sledgehammer (for safety reasons after a major earthquake). She has been surprised to find herself loving her current career as a psychotherapist-in-training in Santa Cruz, California.

Anna Paganelli "sees writing and therapy as two branches of a single tree: They both involve having faith. Faith that each of us matters, that being whole matters to the universe; and faith that if we tell our stories truthfully, we change the direction of our own lives."

RAINER MARIA RILKE (1875–1926) was born in Prague. His parents sent young Rilke, an only child, to military school, wanting him to become an officer, which was not his calling at all. An uncle helped him flee that fate, and he enrolled in a German school, entering the university in 1895 with the knowledge that he wanted to write. By the time he was nineteen his first collection of poems was published. On a trip to Italy, Rilke met Leo Tolstoy, who influenced his writing. Throughout his lifetime he traveled to Italy, Spain, Egypt, and Paris, where he began a new style of poetry inspired by visual art. During his working life Rilke woke up each morning, got dressed in a shirt and tie, ate breakfast, and began to write. He treated writing poems as a job for which he needed to arrive prepared and on time. The last years of his life were spent in Switzerland, where he wrote his famous *Duino Elegies* and *Sonnets to Orpheus*. Upon his death his poetry was known and well regarded, but not nearly to the extent that it is now.

Translator Steven Lautermilch writes, "'Dear Neighbor God' was written in 1899 after Rilke visited Tolstoy; it is set in the voice of a Russian monk. Rilke makes the connection between the divine and the human in an exchange—one neighbor to another. In Rilke's poem, God needs the human, needs human men and women, in order to be divine. It's a give and take. Prayer becomes an opening to a sharing relationship. The faith is in the need." Rainer Maria Rilke wrote, "Religion is art for those who are not creative. They become productive in prayer: they form their love and their gratitude and their longing and thus gain freedom."

SELECTED READING
Letters to a Young Poet (W. W. Norton)
Selected Poetry of Rainer Maria Rilke (translated by Stephen Mitchell; Vintage)
The Wisdom of Rilke (edited and translated by Ulrich Baer; Modern Library)

THEODORE ROETHKE (1908–1963) was born in Michigan, where his parents owned a greenhouse, and Roethke spent much time there as a child, experiences which inspired his poetry. His writing career began early; a speech he wrote for the Junior Red Cross was translated and published in twenty-six languages. When Roethke was still a teenager, his father died, a loss that deeply affected the poet. The family urged him to become a lawyer, but Roethke knew that wasn't the life for him, and after one semester quit law school. The poet Louise Bogan was a great early supporter of Roethke's writing. His first book of poems took him ten years to write. In 1954 he was awarded the Pulitzer Prize, and he was the recipient of two Guggenheim Fellowships, a Fulbright, and the National Book Award. He taught at various colleges and universities.

Roethke suffered from periods of depression, experiences which he said ultimately enhanced his creativity, allowing him to get to a new level. He was inspired by the Surrealists' stream-of-consciousness writing techniques. He is one of the most widely read twentieth-century American poets. About his poetry Mark Doty writes, "To travel either outward or inward is to encounter the self, and the voyage in either direction is fraught with the possibilities of transcendence, dissolution, or both." Roethke, in his book *On Poetry and Craft*, wrote, "You must believe a poem is a holy thing, a good poem, that is."

SELECTED READING

The Collected Poems of Theodore Roethke (Anchor Books/Doubleday)
On Poetry and Craft (essays; Copper Canyon Press)

ELLIOT RUCHOWITZ-ROBERTS (b. 1936) spent his New York childhood terrified by the anti-Semitism in the United States and by the Holocaust and World War II. When he was three his father changed their surname to Roberts in an effort to protect his family. And, for the most part, it did. Not until the events of September 11, 2001, did he reexamine what it had meant to hide his real name, part of his identity. He says, "I realized that I had lived all those years with a sense of shame about my heritage." Shortly afterward he reclaimed the surname of his birth—Ruchowitz.

Coauthor of *Bowing to Receive the Mountain* and coeditor/co-translator of two works of poetry from the Telugu, Chalam's *Sudha (Nectar)* and *Selected Verses of Vemana,* he has published two chapbooks of poetry and his poems have appeared in various anthologies and journals. About his poem Ruchowitz-Roberts writes, "Too often, we overlook the miracles of everyday life, how, for example, our fingers hold a pen and with that pen write a poem on a sheet of paper. At its best, poetry dispels our doubts about everyday miracles. Even when our world discourages belief in such miracles, poetry can give us the faith necessary to persevere."

SELECTED READING
Bowing to Receive the Mountain: Essays by Lin Jensen and Poems by Elliot Roberts (Sunflower Ink)

RUMI (1207–1273), whose full name was Jelaluddin Rumi, was born in what is now Afghanistan. Threatened by a Mongol invasion, his family fled and settled in Turkey. Rumi's ancestors were scholars and theologians. Until he was in his midthirties, Rumi too followed this path and was a teacher until he met a traveling dervish, Shams of Tabriz, whom Rumi perceived as a manifestation of God. Rumi followed the teachings of Tabriz, becoming a whirling dervish, one who dances as an expression of worship. Translators Coleman Barks and John Moyne write, "In Rumi's poetry there is always the mystery of the pronouns." He could be addressing God, but often the poems sound as though they were written to a lover. Barks and Moyne, in *Open Secret: Versions of Rumi,* go on to say, "The essential power of Rumi's poetry is ecstasy."

SELECTED READING
Essential Rumi (translated by Coleman Barks; HarperSanFrancisco)
The Soul of Rumi: A New Collection of Ecstatic Poems (translated by Coleman Barks; HarperSanFrancisco)

KAY RYAN's (b. 1945) poems are compact—she says she writes poems that are equal to her attention span—but only in size. Wanting to decide whether to devote her life to poetry, Ryan took a cross-country bike ride. She said, "I really found that poetry was taking over my mind." Even after her first books garnered no critical acclaim, she continued to write. When asked in a *Poetry Flash* interview when she began to write, Ryan responded, "I think that I had dallied with it, always. . . . I had a dream when I was a little kid. It was such a striking dream that I never forgot it—I was chasing a piece of paper that had the most beautiful poem in the world on it. And at that time, poetry wasn't even a particular interest of mine." The recipient of a Guggenheim Fellowship and the Ruth Lilly Prize, Ryan has taught remedial English at the College of Marin for many years. In an interview with Salon.com she said, "What poetry does is put more oxygen into the atmosphere. Poetry makes it easier to breathe."

SELECTED READING
Say Uncle (poems; Grove Press)
The Niagara River: Poems (Grove Press)

More is unknown than known about the Greek poet **SAPPHO** (600 B.C.E), who lived on the island of Lesbos in the Aegean Sea. The oldest surviving biographies weren't even written until centuries after her death. On Lesbos there's scant reference to her; only two statues stand. Yet her stature as a poet has lasted for centuries and her work is known and loved throughout the world. Plato considered her the tenth Muse. She lived at a time when the only acceptable activities for women outside the home were limited to religion. Yet she wrote and performed poetry. She was famous during her lifetime. She may have run a school for girls. It is said that young women came from far away to study with her, attracted by her fame. And over many centuries, as women's choices became even more limited, scholars found it difficult to explain Sappho and resorted to referring to her disrespectfully.

Most of what we have of her poetry are fragments. Some poems are known because they were remembered by her contemporaries and passed on to future generations. Her poems were burned at Constantinople and Rome in the year 1073. There's a story that says a girl pulled a bundle of Sappho's poems from the mouth of a dead crocodile. Her poems display a lack of self-consciousness and love for women. During Sappho's time poetry was sung or recited to musical accompaniment. Hers was a new type of poetry, a lyric, called the monody. Little is known about Sappho's family though it is believed she had a daughter named Cleis. About herself, Sappho said, "I am not one of a malignant nature, but have a quiet temper."

SELECTED READING
Sappho: A New Translation (poems; University of California Press)

WILLIAM SHAKESPEARE (c. 1564–1616) is the world's most famous and respected playwright. He was born in England to middle-class parents. It is believed that Shakespeare went to school and studied the classics. His plays were performed at the Globe Theatre, where economic status determined where playgoers sat. Shakespeare was a master at creating plays that could be understood and enjoyed on multiple levels. When he was only fifteen Shakespeare bought a desirable piece of land, and it may be that he purchased this property with money earned from his plays. In 1609, without his permission, a selection of his sonnets was published, exposing intimate feelings that he likely would not have wished to share publicly. The last words he wrote may have been those that appeared on his tombstone, asking for his remains to be undisturbed and cursing anyone who might disinter them.

SELECTED READING
Complete Poems of Shakespeare (Random House)
Complete Works of William Shakespeare (Library of Congress Classics)

PERCY BYSSHE SHELLEY (1792–1827) was an English Romantic poet opposed to conservative values. His poetry reflects the revolutionary ideas of his time. Upon publication of his poem "The Necessity of Atheism," he was expelled from college. Shelley was in disagreement with the idea of compulsory Christianity. After he eloped with a young woman, Shelley's father disinherited him. He was only twenty-two when he published his first significant poem, "Queen Mab," which celebrates atheism, vegetarianism, and free love. Shelley believed in the power of both love and reason, and in the progress of man. His marriage didn't last long, and Shelley spent time traveling with feminist Mary Wollstonecraft, author of *A Vindication of the Rights of Women,* whom he later married. With an inheritance that came from his grandfather, Shelley was able to support himself. His most famous poem, "Ozymandias," was published in 1818. Shelley said, "A man, to be greatly good, must imagine intensely and comprehensively; he must put himself in the place of another and of many others; the pains and pleasures of his species must become his own."

SELECTED READING
The Complete Poems (Modern Library)

CHARLES SIMIC (b. 1938), in an interview with *The Cortland Review,* described his childhood in Belgrade, Yugoslavia: "Germans and the Allies took turns dropping bombs on my head while I played with my collection of lead soldiers on the floor. I would go boom, boom, and then they would go boom, boom." His inspiration to write poetry began as a young man when a classmate was able to attract girls by writing them love poems. In 1953 Simic came to the United States with his family. His first poems were published when he was twenty-one. At twenty-three he was drafted into the U.S. Army. The author of more than sixty books, he has received a Pulitzer Prize, a MacArthur Foundation Fellowship, a Guggenheim Fellowship, and grants from the National Endowment for the Arts and the American Academy of Arts and Letters.

His translations have won him two PEN International Translation Awards. In a review of his most recent book, *My Noiseless Entourage, Booklist* wrote, "Simic's gift is his ability to unite the real with the abstract in poems that lend themselves to numerous interpretations, much like dreams." He's lived in New Hampshire since 1973 and teaches English at the University of New Hampshire.

SELECTED READING
Jackstraws: Poems (poems; Harcourt)
My Noiseless Entourage (poems; Harcourt)
Selected Poems (Gardners Books)

Award-winning author of children's books **MARILYN SINGER** (b. 1948) has written about many characters, including a dog who insists he's not a dog, an armadillo, and detective twins. She writes fiction and nonfiction picture books, juvenile novels and mysteries, young adult fantasies, and poetry. Ms. Singer began writing as a child, inspired by her grandmother, and says that poetry is her favorite form. "Poetry is great for asking those questions that come to you just as you're falling asleep." When she received the acceptance letter for her first children's book, she was so excited that she screamed before even finishing the letter. "A book!" she said. "A published book! I was about to become an author! A children's author! How extraordinary! How fine."

About her poem Ms. Singer writes, "The idea of a balance of forces light and dark in the universe has long fascinated me. I believe that our business—and the business of nature—is to find that balance. My being able to see the light in the dark and the dark in the light is personally important—an ongoing search, as it were—but I also know that the yin/yang balance is ever present, whether or not I can see it. And that, too, gives me comfort."

SELECTED READING
Stay True: Short Stories for Strong Girls (Scholastic)
I Believe in Water: Twelve Brushes with Religion (HarperCollins)

Make Me Over: Eleven Original Stories About Transforming Our-
    selves (Dutton)
Central Heating: Poems About Fire and Warmth (Knopf)

The author of three books of poems, **JOSEPH STROUD** (b. 1943)
lives part of the year in Santa Cruz, along the central California
coast, and part of the year in a cabin at Shay Creek, a remote area
in the eastern Sierra Nevada. One of his first poems was a Mother's
Day gift, and upon reading it his mom cried. Stroud says, "I didn't
think much of it at the time, but somewhere it lodged in me that
words have a certain power that moves people." He's a recipient of
the 2006 Witter Bynner Fellowship. For thirty-five years Stroud
taught English at Cabrillo College in Aptos, California, where his
poetry workshop was a favorite among students and local poets.

SELECTED READING
Below Cold Mountain (poems; Copper Canyon)
Country of Light (poems; Copper Canyon)

Born on the Jewish North Side of Chicago, **ROBERT SWARD**
(b. 1933) began writing poetry when he was fifteen. Sward has
been many things in his life thus far: sailor, amnesiac, university
professor, newspaper editor, food reviewer, father of five children,
and husband to four wives; his writing career has been described by
critic Virginia Lee as a "long and winding road." In addition to poetry and fiction, he now produces multimedia "collages" for the
World Wide Web and works as an editorial consultant.

About his poem Robert Sward writes, "Most people, I believe,
are so marked by what occurred in their passage from, say, age
twelve to fifteen, that on an emotional level, at the very core of
their being, that is who they are and will remain all their lives. This
is especially true in matters of doubt and faith. As someone who, at
age twelve, studied Hebrew in preparation for his bar mitzvah, I
learned that language is mystery, that prayer—performed with or
without language—is mystery, and that, as my father said, 'God is

in the cracks.' You misuse or mispronounce words at your peril. As Dad said, 'Jews got souls when they got Torah.' Torah is a rendering of God's word. Torah is soul. Torah is language. I was a skeptic. I had my doubts, but kept them largely to myself. My father was annoyed that I preferred not to go to Hebrew school. For him, an Orthodox Jew, my reluctance to learn, my skepticism and doubt meant I was an apostate, someone who, in effect, was not a Jew at all. I began in doubt, learned enough Hebrew to get through the ceremony. Truth is, as a poet, every reading I give is something of a bar mitzvah. I no longer go to temple and am not religious in any traditional sense. Certainly I've learned to love and respect language. The seeds for that were planted in the late 1940s. All these years later I am as awed by language as I was at age twelve. Language is light; language, for me, is life itself."

SELECTED READING
The Collected Poems of Robert Sward 1957–2004 (Black Moss Press)
Heavenly Sex (poetry; Black Moss Press)

MAY SWENSON (1919–1989), the author of many books of poems, grew up in Utah and received her B.A. from Utah State University. Her first book came out when she was forty-five. She taught poetry at several universities and gave readings of her work at over fifty universities. In addition to being a writer, she was also an editor, critic, and scholar. Swenson received much acclaim for her writing, including a MacArthur Fellowship. Her poems are surprising in their use of wordplay and how they look on the page, not all flush left, but with words moving across and down the page.

May Swenson said that for her, writing was "based in a craving to get through the curtains of things as they appear, to things as they are, and then into the larger, wilder space of things as they are becoming." In her poem "The Centaur" included here, Swenson captures and returns the feeling of summer's lingering, one familiar to many children: "The summer that I was ten— / Can it be there was only one / summer that I was ten? It must / have been a long one then—"

SELECTED READING
The Complete Love Poems of May Swenson (Mariner Books)
Nature: Poems Old and New (Mariner Books)

WISLAWA SZYMBORSKA (b. 1923) was seventy-three when she won the Nobel Prize in 1996. Until then her poetry was little known outside her native Poland. This recognition brought her work great attention, making her a surprise literary star. She is the author of more than fifteen books of poems. Szymborska was born in western Poland and has made her home in Krakow since 1931. She has worked as poetry editor and columnist for the Krakow literary weekly. In 1948 she completed her first collection of poetry, but the book went unpublished because the communist government considered her poetry too bourgeois. She went back to her poems, making them more political, and the book was published. Szymborska became disillusioned with communism, which instilled great fear in the people. Her poetry has become more personal, less political, though she's said, "Apolitical poems are political too." Since winning the Nobel Prize she moved to a quieter area to get away from reporters, saying, "I'm a private person." She has been described as modest to the point of shyness. In his introduction to her book *Monologue of a Dog,* Billy Collins writes, "[B]ecause her imagination is so lively and far-reaching—acrobatic, really—we are led, almost unaware, into the intriguing and untranslatable realms that lie just beyond the boundaries of speech."

Accepting the Nobel Prize, Ms. Szymborska said, "[I]nspiration is not the exclusive privilege of poets or artists generally. There is, has been, and will always be a certain group of people whom inspiration visits. It's made up of all those who've consciously chosen their calling and do their job with love and imagination. It may include doctors, teachers, gardeners—and I could list a hundred more professions. Their work becomes one continuous adventure as long as they manage to keep discovering new challenges in it. Difficulties and setbacks never quell their curiosity. A swarm of new questions emerges from every problem they solve. Whatever inspiration is, it's born from a continuous 'I don't know.'"

SELECTED READING

Monologue of a Dog (poems; translated by Stanislaw Barańczak and Clare Cavanagh; Harcourt)

View with a Grain of Sand: Selected Poems (translated by Stanislaw Barańczak and Clare Cavanagh; Harcourt)

Palestinian poet **FADWA TUQAN** (1917–2003) expressed her nation's sense of loss and defiance in her writing. Referred to as the poet of love and pain, she was deeply beloved by her people. Tuqan is considered one of the best avant-garde poets in the Arab world. She came of age at a time when young, educated Palestinian women and men could spend time together. In her autobiography she describes the difficulty of being a woman in Arab society. At Oxford University, Tuqan studied English language and literature. She was thirty when her first collection of poetry was published. She is the author of nine books of poetry and an autobiography, *A Mountainous Journey.* Israeli general Moshe Dayan compared reading Tuqan's poems to facing twenty enemy commandos. The great power of her words is not only her anger but also their affirmation of the Palestinian identity and the grief at the loss of their land. Tuqan wrote, "I ask nothing more / Than to die in my country / to dissolve and merge with the grass." Her reputation became international in the 1980s when her poetry was translated. An essay in the newspaper *Al Jahid* says, "She was a mother before giving birth, and found herself fighting before loving in spite of herself."

MALKA HEIFETZ TUSSMAN (1896–1987) is one of the best
known Yiddish women poets. In translator Marcia Falk's introduction to a collection of Tussman's poetry, she relays a story Tussman
told. As a young child, "I spoke the language of the owl that made
its nest above our roof. . . . I would hide in the tall stalks of wheat
and listen as they made words." Tussman conversed with the natural world, making up words that sounded like those of the owl or
the breeze. Her first poem was written in these words. When her
father saw it, he was encouraging and said, "Leave her alone. These
are her words. We don't understand." Tussman attended a Russian
school, becoming familiar with the work of such Russian poets as
Anna Akhmatova and Alexander Pushkin. She was sixteen when,
like other Jews of her generation, she had to flee her home, the
Ukrainian province of Volhynia. With her family she came to the
United States. In 1919 when her work first appeared, it was published in Yiddish journals. She wrote for the anarchist journal
Alarm. Her first book of poems came out in 1949 in the United
States. Several subsequent books were published in Israel. In 1981
she was awarded the Itsik Manger Prize, the most prestigious Yiddish literary award. In one of her poems, Tussman speaks of poetry's importance: "Poetry is hunger. Poetry is thirst."

Spanish author and philosopher **MIGUEL DE UNAMUNO**
(1864–1936) was quite influential in early-twentieth-century
Spain. The violence of the siege of Bilbao that he had witnessed as

a child left a deep impression. A highly educated man, he spoke fourteen languages and was a professor at the University of Salamanca. Although his first language was Basque, Unamuno wrote in Spanish. He and his wife, Concepción, had ten children. Because of his opposition to the dictatorship in power, he was exiled from Spain, lived several years in France, and did not return to Spain until 1931, following Miguel Primo de Rivera's death. In 1936 Unamuno was put under house arrest for his denouncement of Francisco Franco's regime. Unamuno died in 1936, shortly after the outbreak of the Spanish Civil War. He is the author of philosophy, poetry, fiction, and plays. Best known for his philosophic writing, he explored the contradiction between reason and Christian faith, religion and the freedom of thought. He encouraged the people of Spain to question and express the value of having differing beliefs. Unamuno said, "Faith which does not doubt is dead faith."

About writing Unamuno said, "The matter of writing is a painful road. You end up being and meditating on those undesirable places and peoples that have been making your life's collage. Yes, this is the writer's work—a bit spacious, but never so lonely."

SELECTED READING
Tragic Sense of Life (philosophy; Dover)
Three Exemplary Novels (Grove)

PATRICE VECCHIONE (b. 1957) is the author of *Writing and the Spiritual Life: Finding Your Voice by Looking Within* and a book of poems, *Territory of Wind*. She is the editor of three previous anthologies for young adults. *Whisper & Shout: Poems to Memorize* is an anthology for children. For nearly thirty years Vecchione has taught poetry to children and adults in schools, libraries, and community centers through her program The Heart of the Word. She gives readings and workshops around the country and is a frequent speaker on writing as a spiritual practice and teaching poetry to children. Additionally, she's a collage artist who loves turning throwaway scraps of paper into pictures. Vecchione lives with her husband in Monterey, California. Her Web site is www.patricevecchione.com.

"Throughout my childhood, out walking New York and Chicago streets with my father, he spent more time looking down than looking around. It was a bit of an embarrassment. But the joke was on me when, years later, I saw how his small change had transformed into bounty—jars full of money! Nearly enough for the down payment on a house. All along, however, I did enjoy the fruits of his willingness to bend down and pick something off the sidewalk—not only the watch in my poem, but cool objects—butterfly wings; shiny, curlicued metal bits; rocks with swirls of color. Until recently, whenever he found money, he slipped that into his own pocket. Now he hands the money over to me. If I see even a penny on the ground and attempt to walk by, the tug at my heart is unbearable. I go back, pick up the penny, and enjoy the moment, thinking of my father. It's a lot like writing poetry, really. Poems are everywhere around us, if we take notice of the small things. What some might miss or turn away from may be treasure to the poet."

SELECTED READING
The Body Eclectic: An Anthology of Poems (Henry Holt)
Revenge and Forgiveness: An Anthology of Poems (Henry Holt)
Truth and Lies: An Anthology of Poems (Henry Holt)
Writing and the Spiritual Life: Finding Your Voice By Looking Within
   (Contemporary/McGraw-Hill)

RONALD WALLACE (b. 1945) is the author of several books of poetry and short fiction. His most recent poetry collections are *The Uses of Adversity* and *Long for This World*. About his work *Publishers Weekly* wrote, "Part of what sets Wallace apart from other poets who write about personal and family life is his virtuosity with complex forms." Wallace is the codirector of the creative writing program at the University of Wisconsin, Madison, and poetry editor for the University of Wisconsin Press. He divides his time between Madison and his forty-acre farm in Bear Valley, Wisconsin.

"Poems are sometimes prayers," writes Ronald Wallace about his poem "The Faithful," "and if I have faith in anything it is the power of language to soothe and woo, to bless and heal. But poems are sometimes rapiers, instruments of doubt and despair. I think my poem is a bit of both."

SELECTED READING
Long for This World: New and Selected Poems (University of Pittsburgh Press)
The Uses of Adversity (poetry; University of Pittsburgh Press)

CHARLES HARPER WEBB's (b. 1952) sixth book of poems, *Amplified Dog,* won the Benjamin Saltman Prize. In addition to being a poet, for fifteen years Mr. Webb was a rock guitarist. A recipient of grants from the Whiting and Guggenheim foundations, he directs the MFA program at California State University, Long Beach. Webb writes, " 'The Death of Santa Claus' sprang into my mind as a verbal cartoon: Santa dying of a heart attack. Then, as sometimes happens, the work seemed to take over, tapping something much deeper than I'd originally had in mind. I wound up with a poem that mourns, in a quirky way, the loss of my belief in Santa—a belief which, up to that time, had infused my life with magic, and made me feel luckier than my cynical eight-year-old peers."

SELECTED READING
Amplified Dog (poems; Red Hen Press)
Hot Popsicles (poems; University of Wisconsin Press)
Reading the Water (poems; University Press of New England)

Of his childhood **WALT WHITMAN** (1819–1892) said, "The time of my boyhood was a very restless and unhappy one; I did not know what to do." His biographer David S. Reynolds believes

Whitman was in a sour mood when he said that, as he noted happy times as well. However, Whitman's early life had its difficulties. His father was professionally unsuccessful and the family upset by the social upheaval of the times. Whitman began learning the trade of printing and worked as a printer in New York. At seventeen he became a teacher in a one-classroom school. Later he turned to journalism and founded a weekly newspaper. Moving to New Orleans a few years later, he became the editor of a paper there. In New Orleans, Whitman experienced firsthand the viciousness of slavery in the slave markets, and this affected him greatly. During the Civil War he worked as a war correspondent and a government clerk. He devoted much of his time to caring for sick and injured soldiers. Whitman would go to the hospitals in Washington, D.C., with gifts for the soldiers—fruit, candy, tobacco, books, pencils, and paper. His visits brought the injured men friendship and comfort. About this experience he said, "I only gave myself."

Whitman's poetry was revolutionary; he liberated poetry by writing in a nonrhyming free verse and rhythmic style that was significantly different from the poetry of the time, which was marked by strict rhyme and meter. In 1855 Whitman self-published his book *Leaves of Grass,* which consisted of twelve untitled poems and a preface. Throughout his life he continued to refine and develop this book, publishing several editions. *Leaves of Grass* is considered a masterpiece of world literature.

In response to the scientific perspective, Whitman wrote, "Your facts are useful, yet they are not my dwelling." He turned to religion and philosophy to gain a deeper understanding of the world and human behavior. Whitman believed the worlds of nature and the spirit to be closely aligned. His was a spirituality of poetry.

SUGGESTED READING

Walt Whitman: The Complete Poems (edited by Francis Murphy; Viking Press)

Walt Whitman's America: A Cultural Biography (by David S. Reynolds; Vintage Books)

English poet **SIR THOMAS WYATT** (1503–1542) spent much of his life in the service of King Henry VIII, except when he was out of favor and imprisoned in the Tower of London, suspected of being a lover to the king's wife Anne Boleyn, and later for charges of treason. He was knighted in 1535. Though he shared his poems with friends, it was not until after his death that they were published.

SELECTED READING
Selected Poems of Sir Thomas Wyatt (Routledge)

AL YOUNG (b. 1939) was born on the Gulf Coast of Mississippi and grew up in the South and Detroit. In 1961 he moved to Berkeley, where he worked as a folksinger, lab aide, disc jockey, and medical photographer before graduating from the University of California at Berkeley. He became a lecturer in creative writing at Stanford University. Young has taught at many colleges and universities. He is the recipient of many honors, including a Guggenheim Fellowship, a Fulbright grant, two American Book Awards, and the Pushcart Prize. His literary work includes novels, collections of poetry, essays, memoirs, and anthologies. He has written film scripts for Bill Cosby, Sidney Poitier, and Richard Pryor. In 2001 he traveled to the Persian Gulf, where he lectured on African-American literature and culture for the U.S. State Department. He's currently Poet Laureate for the State of California. Mr. Young is at work on a new novel titled *A Piece of Cake.*

In an interview with *Metro Santa Cruz* newspaper, Al Young said, "We're going through these dark critical days, which is when poetry always surfaces. Poetry is the original human language. . . . When all you have is your body and voice, poetry is the art form that's still there."

SELECTED READING
Heaven: Collected Poems 1956–1990 (Creative Arts Book Company)
Mingus/Mingus: Two Memoirs (with Janet Coleman; Limelight Editions)

Poet, artist, and editor **GARY YOUNG**'s (b. 1951) book *Braver Deeds* won the Peregrine Smith Poetry Prize. Young has received fellowships from the National Endowment for the Arts and the National Endowment for the Humanities. His print work is represented in many collections, including the Museum of Modern Art and the Getty Center for the Arts. He's the editor of the Greenhouse Review Press. Young makes his home in the Santa Cruz Mountains in northern California. Gary Young writes, "My poem is derived from an unexpected revelation: that anger and pain can sometimes bring their opposites, love and forgiveness, into a sharper focus."

SELECTED READING

The Geography of Home: California's Poetry of Place (editor, with Christopher Buckley; Heyday Books)
No Other Life (poems; Heyday Books)
Pleasure (poems; Heyday Books)

SAADI YOUSSEF (b. 1934), one of the leading poets of the Arab world, was born in Basra, Iraq. The internationally known author of thirty collections of poetry and several books of prose, Youssef began writing poetry when he was seventeen. In 1979 he left Iraq and now makes his home in London. Poet Marilyn Hacker writes, "Saadi Youssef was born in Iraq, but he has become, through the vicissitudes of history and the cosmopolitan appetites of his mind, a poet, not only of the Arab world, but of the human universe." He has translated many significant poets from English into Arabic, and his own poetry has been translated into several languages. He was invited to give a reading in the United States in 2005; despite his stature, the U.S. government denied Youssef a visa.

SELECTED READING

Without an Alphabet, Without a Face: Selected Poems (translated by Khaled Mattawa; Graywolf Press)

Permissions

"The Place Where We Are Right" by Yehuda Amichai from *The Selected Poetry of Yehuda Amichai,* University of California Press. Translated by Chana Bloch and Stephen Mitchell. Copyright © 1996 by Yehuda Amichai. Reprinted by permission of Hana Amichai.

"The Dirty Hand" by Carlos Drummond de Andrade. Translated by Mark Strand from *Reasons for Moving, Darker, and The Sargentville Notebook: Poems.* Translation copyright © 1973 by Mark Strand. Reprinted by permission of Alfred A. Knopf, a division of Random House, Inc.

"Not" by Joy Castro. Copyright © 2007 by Joy Castro. Used by permission of author.

"Echoes" by John Ciardi from *The Collected Poems of John Ciardi,* edited by Edward M. Cifelli. Copyright © 1989 by the Ciardi Family Publishing Trust. Reprinted by permission of the University of Arkansas Press, www.uapress.com.

"praise song" by Lucille Clifton from *Blessing the Boats: New and Selected Poems 1988–2000.* Copyright © 2000 by Lucille Clifton. Reprinted by permission of Boa Editions, Ltd. www.BOAEditions.org.

"Yet Do I Marvel" by Countee Cullen from *Color.* Copyright © 1925, renewed 1952, by Ida M. Cullen. Reprinted by permission of Amistad Research Center, Tulane University, administered by Thompson and Thompson, Brooklyn, NY.

"My worthiness is all my doubt" by Emily Dickinson from *The Poems of Emily Dickinson,* edited by Thomas H. Johnson, Belknap Press of Harvard University, Cambridge, Mass. Copyright © 1951, 1955, 1979, 1983 by the President and Fellows of Harvard College. Reprinted by permission of the publishers and Trustees of Amherst College, Harvard University Press.

"The Girl Who Loved the Sky" by Anita Endrezze from *at the helm of twilight.* Copyright © 1992 by Anita Endrezze. Reprinted by permission of the author.

"My Grandfather's Hat" by Nicholas Gardner. Copyright © 2007 by Nicholas Gardner. Used by permission of the author.

"God Says Yes to Me" by Kaylin Haught from *In the Palm of Your Hand: The Poet's Portable Handbook* by Steve Kowitt. Copyright © 1995. Reprinted by permission of Kaylin Haught.

"The Berries" by William Heyen from *Shoah Train: Poems.* Copyright © 2004 by William Heyen. Reprinted by permission of the author and Etruscan Press.

"The Direction of Light" by Linda Hogan from *The Book of Medicines.* Copyright © 1993 by Linda Hogan. Reprinted by permission of Coffee House Press, Minneapolis, MN.

"Doubt" by Sara Holbrook from *I Never Said I Wasn't Difficult* (Wordsong, an imprint of Boyds Mills Press). Copyright © 1996 by Sara Holbrook. Reprinted by permission of Boyds Mills Press, Inc.

"Watch god crumble" by Akasha Gloria Hull. Copyright © 2007 by Akasha Gloria Hull. Used by permission of the author.

"Long Drop to Black Water" by Judy Jordan from *Carolina Ghost Woods: Poems.* Copyright © 2000 by Judy Jordan. Reprinted by permission of Louisiana State University Press.

Index of Authors